MW01282478

A Man Called
KING

The Life and Legacy of King Turpin, Jr.

J. Randolph Turpin, Jr.

THE HOLY BIBLE, NEW INTERNATIONAL VERSION®, NIV® Copyright © 1973, 1978, 1984, 2010 by Biblica, Inc.™ Used by permission. All rights reserved worldwide.

This material may not be reproduced in any form without the expressed written permission of the author.

For further information, contact:

J. Randolph Turpin, Jr.
jrturpin2010@gmail.com
http://turpintree.blogspot.com

Copyright © 2010 by J. Randolph Turpin, Jr.
All Rights Reserved

To
my children,
Tiffany, Miranda,
Benjamin, Alycia, Moriah,
their children,
and their children's children

Contents

Preface

Sitting on the front porch of his home on the outskirts of Kansas, Ohio, King Turpin played his guitar, sang silly songs and laughed with his grandchildren. I was one of them. Occasionally he would cease from his jesting and start talking about his journey of faith. Even then I was fascinated by his stories, but how I wish I had asked more questions.

In 1977, the same year as King's death, the television miniseries, *Roots*, aired. As I watched night after night this story about the generations of an Afro-American family, my curiosity was stirred. Could I possibly pull together the story of the Turpin family by researching my own roots?

My search began. Grandpa Turpin was no longer with us, and he seldom volunteered to say much about his own childhood or ancestry while he was living. No one seemed to know much about the years preceding King's arrival in the mountains of West Virginia. Were those stories lost to time?

When my father took note of my intense interest, he told me of his great aunt, Laura Turpin, who was still living somewhere in the Knox County, Tennessee area. I had never heard of her. Dad thought that she might be a good source for information on the early days of my grandfather's life.

When I first met Laura in 1980, she was ninety-nine years old. Yes, she was a great source for family history information, but I could hardly keep her on the subject at hand. She kept "side-tracking" the conversation by initiating talk about serving the Lord. She spoke of salvation and sanctification—the call to a holy life. It was in the midst of these deviations from my interview questions that I realized that I was in the presence of the very person who was responsible for my grandfather's faith in God.

After interviewing Laura, other interviews were arranged. I had the opportunity to meet two people that few of us in my generation even knew existed. I met Minnie Belle Turpin Hall, my grandfather's sister, and Ida Belle Conatser Turpin, my grandfather's step-mother.

Transcripts from these interviews were typed out and circulated through a newsletter that I called, *The Turpin Tree.* Circulation of these stories stirred up memories among relatives of other pieces of oral tradition that were almost forgotten. Library research combined with the compilation of these fragments eventually led to the production of a photocopied "book" generated using Family Tree Maker software.

Then came the Internet. A massive amount of information poured in, but the process of verifying all of the data was overwhelming. Knowing that I had other responsibilities in life other than genealogy, for a time, I packed it all away and addressed other more pressing matters.

In 2008, I took up the hobby once again. Launching the *Turpin Tree* blog site attracted many more people who seemed to share my passion for the family story. But what was I going to do with all of this information? What good would come from all of this effort? It was then that I decided something needed to be published out of this work.

Writing about the full span of Turpin history would have been too much to handle at that time. I soon came to settle on what started this pursuit in the first place. It all started with my grandfather, King Turpin, sitting on the front porch telling his stories. This book is about him.

This final work is the product of over fifty years of listening to family stories and observing the fruit of this man's life. Yes, these pages are a *tribute* to him, but hopefully the reader will find this collection of memories, stories and histories to be inspirational as well. It is also hoped that researchers studying other lines of the East Tennessee Turpins will find this document to be a useful resource; an index has been provided at the end to facilitate such use of the text.

Although great care has been taken to be accurate, some details have been intentionally omitted to protect the privacy of living relatives. If other details have been inadvertently missed, reader feedback on such items will be considered in the event that a second edition is ever attempted.

I am grateful to so many who have helped to make this work possible. First, I must acknowledge the contributions of those who are no longer among us: Laura Caldonia Turpin Dunaway, Minnie Belle Turpin Hall, and Ida Belle Conatser Turpin. Then there are the several conversations that I have had with my grandmother, Bertha Lee Church Green—"Green" by her second marriage after Grandpa Turpin's death.

A distant cousin, John Strunk, is to be credited for opening a treasure house of information related to the generations preceding King. My father, Jim Turpin, and my aunt, Alice Turpin Hatfield, have related stories from their childhood years with their Dad. Many thanks are especially due to my father who conducted a number of interviews with his siblings and his mother, Bertha. He also proofed the rough draft of the manuscript, searching for inaccuracies.

My whole household has been involved in one way or another. My daughter, Miranda, has walked through a number of cemeteries with me, taking photographs and helping me to process data. She has also cranked through hundreds of yards of scratched up microfilm at the East Tennessee History Center in Knoxville. My daughter, Alycia, has provided a transcript of an interview that she conducted with my father a year or so ago for a school project. My wife, Kerry Joy King Turpin, has proofed and copyedited the text. (If there are still errors, they are probably my fault due to additions I have made following Kerry's completed work. She is very thorough.) My other children, Tiffany, Benjamin and Moriah, have been dialog partners, and they have been very patient and understanding while waiting for Dad to finish his book.

Countless others have provided information through emails, letters, blog posts, phone calls and Facebook posts. It would be impossible to name them all. I deeply appreciate all who have helped. Many of them have been credited in the footnotes of the text.

As I am typing this preface, I am sitting in the home of my daughter, Tiffany Michelle Turpin Zajas, in Nashville, Tennessee. It is Thanksgiving Day. My wife, my other four children and my son-in-law are here as well. Half of the family is sleeping someplace in the house after having eaten a tremendous Thanksgiving meal. Later, Tiffany's husband, Jonathan, and I will go over details related to the cover design for this book. The other parts of the manuscript are now complete. All that remains are the next few lines and the Contents page. It is all coming together. Not only is the book coming together, but life is coming together as it is supposed to be with the family that surrounds me. Why is that so? A treasure of eternal worth has been passed on to this family. It is the legacy of King Turpin, Jr. May the reader read and comprehend the riches that may be found in a life wholeheartedly devoted to God.

J. Randolph Turpin, Jr.
Thanksgiving Day
November 25, 2010

Chapter 1

Life in East Tennessee

One hundred fifty years of the Turpin family story follows the Tennessee River and its tributaries. In the winter of 1779-1780, Nathan and Solomon Turpin penetrated the frontier, joining John Donelson's flotilla down the Tennessee and up the Cumberland. Between 1797 and 1805, Martin Turpin of Virginia—the first of the East Tennessee Turpins—arrived in Knox County, Tennessee by raft on the Clinch—a river that originates in Virginia and meets the Tennessee at present-day Kingston. Martin, as well as his son, James, farmed along the north side of the Clinch, and three of Martin's grandsons swam across this river to flee from the Confederates and join the Union Army. The saga continues with Martin Turpin's great-grandson, Joshua King Turpin, finding his livelihood on the Tennessee River in 1902.

Riches to Rags

Born out of wedlock in the 1870's as the son of an affluent Roane County, Tennessee man named Joshua King Christenberry, Joshua King Turpin had known days of plenty. By court order, Joshua King's mother, Serelda, had received support from Mr. Christenberry. She had also been supported by Frank Hardin, presumably the father of her second son, Frank. Years later Serelda's daughter, Laura, reported, "You see, our mother never was married. She just stayed around here with these rich folks and had children by them. We had money, as far as that went."[1]

Serelda and her sister, Amanda, both lived a deviant and self-indulgent lifestyle. Although most decent folks shunned them, Serelda and Amanda reveled in the luxuries afforded them by the wealthy men they had ensnared. Amanda was known to take train trips to the city, returning with trunk loads of new expensive items of clothing. For a number of years, a large portrait of Amanda existed which showed her to be a finely dressed woman with a large feathery hat.[2]

For Serelda, the situation drastically changed overnight when King Christenberry terminated his support. This unforeseen hardship combined with other tragic circumstances quickly forced this single-parent family into a state of homelessness.[3] For awhile, Serelda and her

[1] Interview with Laura Turpin Dunaway, about 1980.

[2] Interview with John Strunk, about 1997.

[3] The additional adverse circumstances included, among other factors, an unresolved dispute over land ownership. After Serelda's father, James Turpin, had died, her mother, Jerusa, released control of the family's property to her son William. Shortly thereafter, William was murdered. Within months, his widow also died, and the property fell into the hands of the guardians of William's children. Jerusa fought in the courts for compensation, but the situation was never resolved. Jerusa's

children—Joshua King, Laura and Frank—wandered as vagrants until they eventually settled in Hardin Valley south of the Clinch River.

They had no money, and for the longest time they had no place they could call their own. However, years later Laura Turpin was careful to note that she and her siblings did know what it was like to experience a mother's love.[4] Serelda loved her children. Such was the childhood world of Joshua King Turpin.

King Enters Adulthood

From childhood, Joshua King Turpin was known by the name "King." Once he matured and launched out on his own, King eventually made his home in Anderson County, Tennessee.

As far as anyone knows, no photographs of Joshua King Turpin have survived. Those who knew him describe him as a small man in stature. He was intelligent and skilled. In his sister Laura's opinion, "He was smart—too smart!"[5] Farming was his primary vocation, but he also refinished furniture,

---

indebtedness for legal and court fees resulted in court orders to confiscate whatever little possessions she and her family had remaining. In a short time, Jerusa died, and Serelda together with her children were expelled from their home. Based on a synthesis of court documents and an Interview with Laura Turpin Dunaway, about 1980.

[4] Ibid.

[5] Ibid.

painted houses and worked on watches, clocks, guns and organs. In his final years, he worked as a projectionist in a movie theatre.

The Next Generation

On August 3, 1895, King married a woman named Sarah Morrow in Anderson County.[6] King's brother, Frank, signed the marriage certificate as a witness, signing with an "x." In 1898 the next generation began; Sarah gave birth to a daughter named Rosie,[7] also known as "Rosa."[8] However, King and Sarah did not remain together long. In 1898, the same year that Rosie was born, King was in a relationship with Elizabeth Belle Magsby.[9]

**King Turpin's signature on the marriage certificate
for his marriage to Sarah Morrow**

---

[6] "Tennessee State Marriages, 1780-2002," Ancestry.com, http://www.ancestry.com (accessed November 11, 2010).

[7] Someone has stated that Rosie was named after one of King's sisters.

[8] "1910 United States Federal Census," Ancestry.com, http://www.ancestry.com (accessed November 11, 2010).

[9] Elizabeth Belle Magsby's last name may have been McBee. The family name, Magsby, appears to be rare—even non-existent—in the Knox, Roane and Anderson County area during this period. However, the McBee family name does appear frequently.

Her preferred name was Belle. Sometimes people called her Lizzy. One source recalls that Belle was a young woman with long blonde hair.[10] In May of 1899, she gave birth to King's first son--William McKinley Magsby. King and Belle were not yet married

Amanda Turpin

In 1900, King, Belle and their son, William, were living with Aunt Mandy (Amanda Turpin) in Anderson County. Belle was Mandy's servant. Where was Sarah? She was living at the county asylum for the poor with her two-year old daughter, Rosie.[11]

By 1902 King had acquired a houseboat. Being a man of many skills, he installed a steam engine on the boat, enabling him to travel up and down the Tennessee River. As King found work along the river, he and Belle would find a mooring where they could secure their boat

---

[10] Interview with Minnie Belle Turpin Hall, abt. 1981.

[11] 1900 United States Federal Census, Anderson County, Tennessee" Ancestry.com, http:///www.ancestry.com (accessed November 11, 2010). The Anderson County poor farm was located at the site of what was formerly the Bradley farm five miles south of Clinton in the old Fourth Civil District on the Clinch River where it crosses the mouth of Blockhouse Valley. Katherine Baker Hoskins, "Second Poorhouse Built in 1895," The Poorhouse Story, http://poorhousestory.com/TN_ANDERSON_History_p156_Sept30_1976.htm (accessed November 11, 2010).

and stay in that place until the job was done. It was in these days on the river that Belle became pregnant—another child was on the way.

Birth on the River

On February 3, 1903 Belle gave birth to a son on the houseboat while it was moored in Chattanooga, Tennessee.[12] The child would bear his father's name; they called him "Little King."[13] The story conveyed through these pages is about this child who would one day become the man called King.

To place the time of Little King's birth in historical context, it should be noted that he was born thirty-eight years after the end of the Civil War. Theodore Roosevelt was the President. Harry Houdini—the escape artist—was a popular performer. Due to a drought, Niagara Falls was about to run out of water. Later that year, the first cross-country automobile trip was completed from San Francisco to New York. Ford motor company was incorporating, and near the end of 1903, Orville Wright would complete the first sustained motorized flight at Kitty Hawk, North Carolina.

---

[12] Social Security records indicate a birth date of February 3, 1903. However, some have suggested that he may have been born on February 2 in either 1902 or 1903.

[13] In May of 1899 a son named William McKinley Magsby was born to King and Belle. It is unknown whether or not the child was still living at the time of Little King's birth.

Life on the River

Little King's earliest memories were among the people of the river. It is not known how far his family journeyed down this river system that leads to the Ohio and Mississippi, but it is known that they did stay in northern Alabama for awhile. While still living on the boat, three or four years after Little King's birth, Belle gave birth to another child someplace in Alabama. On March 1, 1906 a daughter was born. They named her Minnie Belle.

In time, Fred Dewey Turpin was also born to King and Belle. Another girl was born as well, but she died before she could be given a name. While information about Little King and Minnie Belle abounds, little is known about their two brothers, William and Fred. All that is known is that they died at a very young age. Their half-sister, Rosie, shows up later as the grandmother of seven sets of twins.[14] Rosie lived until 1977.

---

[14] Later in life, Rosie married Charles Raby, and they had a daughter named Amanda Jane Raby Pearson. The author first learned of Amanda through Aunt Laura Turpin Dunaway who reported that her niece, Amanda, had seven sets of twins plus several other children! According to Time Magazine's website, with the birth of Amanda's seventh consecutive set of twins on July 21, 1961, she broke the U.S. record for consecutive births of twins. *Time*, "Milestones: July 21, 1961," 1961, http:// www.time.com/ time/ magazine/ article/ 0,9171,897850,00.html (accessed November 11, 2010).

The children had a few frightening experiences on the river. Once Little King fell out of the houseboat and could not get back in. He yelled for his mother, but she could not get him. Then the current swept him up under the boat, and he got caught. Someone had to dive in and get him. On another occasion, Little King's father threw him into the river just to teach him how to swim.

Throughout their growing up years, the two children, Little King and Minnie, continued to live in the Tennessee River Valley—either on or near the river. As brother and sister, they remained very close to one another. Minnie sometimes called Little King "Jim." It is not known why she would have referred to her brother by that name.

Aunt Laura and Uncle Frank

King frequently returned with his family to Knox County to visit his brother and sister—Frank and Laura. Frank had purchased 8½ acres from Robert Brashears on Beaver Creek in Hardin Valley for $80. Frank Turpin is the first Turpin on record to have owned land in Knox County.[15]

---

[15] This purchase was made on November 5, 1907. Registry of Deeds, East Tennessee History Center, Knoxville, TN. (Book 218, Page 270). On September 29, 1908, Frank acquired right of way from Sarah Summers for a road known today as "Turpin Lane," leading to Frank's previously purchased property. Registry of Deeds, East Tennessee History Center, Knoxville, TN. (Book 224, Page 102). According to Google Earth, the house on this property was located at latitude 35°56'34.45"N, longitude 84°11'57.53"W.

Although their upbringing had been much less than favorable, during the early 1900's in Knox County, something began to stir within Laura and her brother, Frank, that would forever change the lives of many who would follow in generations to come.

Laura and Frank Turpin

The events leading up to Frank and Laura's personal spiritual encounter are interwoven with a significant chapter of American church history. The man that Little King would one day become was largely due to these happenings. For this reason, the background for what was about to take place in Frank and Laura's life is worth noting.

9

Frank and Laura Turpin's House – Photo taken in 2008

Spiritual Influences from Far Away

Far away in the nation of Wales, a spiritual awakening had begun, due largely to the prayers and ministry of a man named Evan Roberts. One account of the revival reports,

> People were changed in so many ways. The crime rate dropped, drunkards were reformed, pubs reported losses in trade. Bad language disappeared and never returned to the lips of many.... It was reported that the pit ponies failed to understand their born again colliers who seemed to speak the new language of Zion— without curse and blasphemy.... Even football and rugby

became uninteresting in the light of new joy and direction received by the Converts.[16]

When news of the revival crossed the Atlantic, many Christians felt compelled to pray and ask God for a similar work of the Holy Spirit in America. Some even traveled to Wales to witness first-hand the miraculous transformation of lives that was taking place.

By 1905, a number of believers in Los Angeles, California had become convinced that the developments in Wales were part of a move of God toward the fulfilling of Joel 2:23-29—a prophecy that states,

> Be glad, O people of Zion, rejoice in the LORD your God, for he has given you the autumn rains in righteousness. He sends you abundant showers, both autumn and spring rains, as before.
>
> The threshing floors will be filled with grain; the vats will overflow with new wine and oil.
>
> I will repay you for the years the locusts have eaten....
>
> You will have plenty to eat, until you are full, and you will praise the name of the LORD your God, who has worked wonders for you; never again will my people be shamed.
>
> Then you will know that I am in Israel, that I am the LORD your God, and that there is no other; never again will my people be shamed.

---

[16] "The Welsh Revival: A History of 1904 and News of Today," http://www.welshrevival.com (accessed November 11, 2010).

And afterward, I will pour out my Spirit on all people. Your sons and daughters will prophesy, your old men will dream dreams, your young men will see visions. Even on my servants, both men and women, I will pour out my Spirit in those days.

Expectant Christians in Los Angeles began to pray for a visitation of the Holy Ghost;[17] they yearned to have an encounter with God just as believers in Wales had experienced.

Los Angeles had been made ready for revival. In February of 1906, a black minister named William J. Seymour had been invited to preach. He preached about a manifestation of the Holy Ghost known as "speaking in tongues."[18] Seymour had not personally experienced this work of the Spirit, but based on teaching he had received under Charles F. Parham in Houston, Texas, he believed that speaking in tongues was the initial evidence of the baptism in the Holy Ghost.

On April 9, 1906, Seymour was preaching at 214 North Bonnie Brae Street in Los Angeles, and the power of the Holy Ghost fell upon the gathering. On that day it is reported that one man received the baptism in the Holy

---

[17] At the time of this writing, the words "Holy Spirit" are typically preferred rather than "Holy Ghost." However, due to the fact that the words "Holy Ghost" were used more frequently during the period of history being covered, the words "Holy Ghost" will often be used in this text.

[18] See Acts 2 and 1 Corinthians 12-14.

Ghost and began to speak in tongues. On the days that followed, others started receiving the same experience. This move of the Spirit escalated, and the meetings had to be moved to Azusa Street. Thus this awakening became known as the Azusa Street Revival—the beginning of the modern-day Pentecostal movement.[19]

As news of the Azusa Street Revival swept across the nation and around the world, multitudes hungry for revival traveled great distances to attend the meetings. One such

person drawn to the revival was a man named Sam C. Perry. Like so many others, Perry received the baptism in the Holy Ghost and left the Azusa Street meetings eager to carry the Pentecostal message wherever the Lord might lead.

After returning to his home in Fort Myers, Florida, Perry started preaching on the baptism in the Holy Ghost. His ministry took him beyond Florida and on up through the Southeastern states. By late 1906 or

Sam C. Perry

at some point in 1907, Perry found himself carrying the Pentecostal blessing into East Tennessee.

---

[19] A similar outpouring of the Holy Spirit had taken place ten years earlier in 1896 at Camp Creek, North Carolina, among members of the Holiness Church—the group that later became known as the Church of God (Cleveland, Tennessee).

Revival at Chandlers View Baptist Church[20]

In 1906 or 1907, Laura Turpin was among those attending Chandlers View Baptist Church, three miles from her brother Frank's house. The church was located at the present site of Solway Methodist Church cemetery. A revival had broken out there, and a woman named Anna Cagley had received the baptism in the Holy Ghost.[21]

Original Site of Chandlers View Baptist Church

Anna's experience caused quite a stir in the church. Others, including Laura Turpin, began praying and asking the Lord to do the same for them. They even prayed asking

---

[20] Based on information provided by Randy Tinch, an acquaintance of Laura Turpin.

[21] Anne Cagley was born August 25, 1893 and died December 13, 1961. She is buried at Solway Methodist Church cemetery. "Knox County, TN Cemeteries - Solway Methodist Church Cemetery," UsGenWeb Archives, http:// files.usgwarchives.net/ tn/ knox/ cemeteries/ solway.txt (accessed November 11, 2010).

the Lord to send someone to the church who knew something about this Pentecostal experience.

Not long after the group had begun to pray, Sam C. Perry, who had just received the Holy Ghost baptism at the Azusa Street Revival, got off the train at the Solway depot. Without anyone knowing him and without him knowing them, he walked into the Chandlers View church and began to preach about the infilling of the Holy Ghost.

Laura was so hungry for the Lord, but she did not receive the baptism in the Holy Ghost in that service. She went home after the service, got behind the front door in her house and prayed. As she was praying at home, she was filled with the Holy Ghost. According to Randy Tinch, who knew Laura later in her life, the Lord led her over to either a piano or organ that she had in her home, and she sat down. Being full of the Holy Ghost, she started playing the instrument and sang in tongues.[22]

Frank and Laura's Spirituality

Throughout the years that followed, Laura Turpin's testimony was always, "I thank the Lord I am saved, sanctified, and filled with the Holy Ghost with the Bible evidence of speaking in tongues."

From the time Laura gave her heart to God, she felt that she needed to sell out completely to the Lord. Laura would

---

[22] Interview with Randy Tinch, 2010.

always take her Bible and a harmonica with her.[23] She would play hymns. When she would talk to people, she would start talking about salvation. If she found out that they were already saved, she would start talking about sanctification.[24] She saw no need to talk about being baptized in the Holy Ghost. The way she saw it, if you got "good and sanctified," you wouldn't be able to keep the Holy Ghost out.[25]

Often when Laura would start talking about sanctification she would stand up and start shouting.[26] She would clap her hands, rock back and forth, and start bowing almost to her knees.

Although Frank and Laura lived most of their adult life at what most perceived as poverty level, they were very generous people, willing to share whatever they had with

---

[23] Those who knew Laura Turpin referred to the harmonica as a "French harp."

[24] Sanctification is a biblical doctrine characteristic of the Holiness movement. It involves the belief that by God's grace and power, followers of Jesus Christ are enabled to live a life free from the controlling grip of sin.

[25] Based on interviews with Barbara Hendrix, Rose Crawford, Katherine Nauman, and Grace Bowls.

[26] In the classical Holiness-Pentecostal tradition, the term "shout" is often used as a reference to the outward display of emotional and demonstrative worship at points when a person might be overwhelmed by the presence and power of God.

others in need. As God blessed their crops, they gave much of their produce away.[27]

People would come from all over to get Laura to pray for their loved ones who were sick. Not all were healed, but they would get saved. One lady that Laura went to visit was dying and started screaming to get pulled from the flames. She could feel the flames of hell on her feet. Laura led the woman to the Lord, and the woman died, leaving this world with a smile on her face.

Frank and Laura would grow corn and sell it. One time Laura tripped, fell in the corn field and broke her arm. She and Frank set her arm with a card board splint that they made, and they wrapped her arm in cloth. They prayed, and when she got up the next morning, her arm was totally healed. She immediately went out to work in the field.

Laura held to a high standard of holiness. She used to love coffee. She would pour it in a pan, place it on an old wood stove, add water and drink it. God said to her that the coffee was becoming a god to her. She grabbed the handle of that pan and flung it out the back door. She never drank another cup from that day on.

As visitors approached Frank and Laura's house, they could hear them praying. If not in the house, they were

---

[27] Ibid.

praying out in the fields while they worked. They were loved and respected.[28]

God told Frank and Laura to walk from where they lived in Hardin Valley to a place over in Solway under an oak tree. There they would have services. God told them that if they would be faithful, the latter days of the church that would start there would be greater than the beginning.

Frank and Laura's spirituality became a formative influence upon King and Belle's children--Little King and Minnie in particular. Regretfully, adults in the family such as Laura's brother, King, her mother, Serelda, and her aunt, Amanda, were not as receptive. Although Little King lived his childhood years traveling up and down the Tennessee River valley with his father, Providence saw to it that he would be repeatedly drawn back into the godly stabilizing influence of Laura and her brother, Frank.

Belle's Death

Eventually Little King's parents either separated or divorced, and at some point his mother, Belle, met up with a man named John Selby.[29] Little King and Minnie remained with their father and Aunt Mandy (Amanda Turpin). Mandy helped take care of the children.

---

[28] Ibid.

[29] The names "Shelby" and "Silvey" are also possibilities for this man's name.

Shortly after Belle met up with John Selby, she became fatally ill. The year was probably between 1906 and 1910.[30] Belle sent word to King that she wanted to see her children one last time before she died. Family members put straw in a horse-drawn wagon, spread quilts on it, and transported Belle to 525 Market Square or Market Street in Chattanooga where King had rented some rooms. If the address was Market Square, then the rooms may have been rented at a boarding house known as the Delmonico Hotel (later known as Hotel Ross) located at Market Square. If the address was Market Street, then the rooms may have been at or near Silvey Livery.

Little King, who was about five years old, carried in wood for the fire to keep his mother warm. The others worked to make Belle comfortable in the bed they had prepared for her.

Little King's father still loved Belle. John Selby came out of Belle's room, turned to the elder King and said, "Yes, if you want to, go right on in there and see her."

---

[30] According to an interview with Minnie conducted in 1981, Belle was about nineteen years of age at this time. However, uncertain information from census records places her as being born about 1880, meaning that she would have been at least 26 to 30 years of age at the time.

Hotel at the Corner of Market Square

Market Street, Chattanooga, Tennessee in 1909

King, Sr. walked to the foot of the bed, spent a few moments with her and then returned to the other room. Minnie, who was only one year old, was sitting in the baby chair, and Mandy was feeding her breakfast. Little King was sitting at the table.

John stepped back into Belle's room. A few moments passed, and he asked, "Belle, how are you feeling?"

She looked up at him, laughed, closed her eyes, and died.

"King, come here!" John called out.

King stepped in. "Belle is dead," John said.

Little King's father would not believe that Belle was dead, so he called for the doctor.

When the doctor arrived, he went straight into Belle's room, quickly examined her, turned to King and said, "King, what did you send for me for? She's gone."

On that same day, Belle was buried in Beasley graveyard in Chattanooga.[31] King stayed up and put a wire fence around her grave that night.[32]

---

[31] Minnie named the cemetery as Beasley Cemetery; however, this cemetery has not yet been located. Interview with Minnie Belle Turpin Hall, about 1981.

[32] Ibid.

Life Without a Mother

For a period of one to five years (depending on the date of Belle's death), Little King and Minnie lived their lives without the love of a mother.[33] Their father tried his best to raise them alone, but he never seemed to recover from the loss of Belle. Nevertheless, King continued to forge a life for him and his children on the Tennessee River.

One day some of Little King and Minnie's mother's cousins came to their house asking to see a photograph that King had of Belle. Shortly after that visit, those two cousins died. The photograph of Belle was later destroyed in a house fire.[34]

From this point forward in the narrative of Little King's childhood years, the sequence of stories is not certain, for King, Sr. and his children seemed to be continually on the move up and down the Tennessee River valley. When and where some of these events occurred is not always clear. Both Laura and Aunt Mandy helped with the rearing of the children from time to time. There were a few extended periods when the children were solely in Laura's care while King was away working.

---

[33] Research has revealed nothing regarding the whereabouts of King and Belle's other sons, William and Fred.
[34] Ibid.

Lookout Mountain

Growing up as children in Chattanooga, against their father's orders, Little King and Minnie would occasionally run off together to try to climb Lookout Mountain. They would climb its steep slopes and then slide back fifty feet or so. At other times Little King would run off by himself just to ride the Incline up the mountain.[35] The adventure of the ascent, the panoramic view from the summit and the technology of the Incline railway had an allurement that Little King could not resist.

The Incline

Since 1895 this technological marvel, the Incline, had become an indispensable means for reaching residences, businesses and attractions on the summit. The Incline ascended at a maximum grade of 72.7%, making it the steepest passenger railway in the world. If Little King did in fact set out on his runaway adventures prior to 1911, in that period of history the Incline was still driven by huge coal-burning steam engines. The sound and sight of such powerful machines would have certainly captured the imagination of

---

35 Ibid.

a little boy. The Incline converted to electric power after 1911.[36]

Tile Town

A point came when King, Sr. and his children obviously no longer lived on a houseboat. There was a period in which they made their home in two culverts—a couple of drain tiles alongside the river. Minnie described their home as "one of those big concrete things that goes into the river." The place was called "Tile Town."

A lot of fishermen lived there; they had several tiles for each family. The Turpins had two tiles; one was used for storing their meat, and the other was the place where they set up their beds. While living there, Little King and Minnie would go out in a boat to catch drift plants. They would cut up the drift plants and sell them. [37]

The location of Tile Town is uncertain. However, there is an interesting reference to a place by that name in the journal of a Union soldier during the Civil War. On April 20, 1862, John Beatty wrote,

> At Decatur. The Memphis and Charleston Railroad crosses the Tennessee river at this point. Tile town is a

---

[36] "History of the Incline Railway," Lookout Mountain's Incline Railway, http://www.ridetheincline.com (accessed November 11, 2010).

[37] Interview with Minnie Belle Turpin Hall, about 1981.

dilapidated old concern, as ugly as Huntsville is handsome.[38]

Could it be that fifty years later, this place was still known as Tile Town? Possibly. Did the Turpins have any connection with Decatur, Alabama on the Tennessee River? Possibly. It has already been established that they were previously familiar with life on the Tennessee River in northern Alabama; Minnie was born there. However, there is not yet conclusive evidence identifying this Tile Town of 1862 located near the railroad bridge at Decatur as the same as the Turpins' Tile Town of 1906-1916.

A Move to Roane County

By 1910, King and his children were living in Roane County. The census shows that King was farming. At that time, Rosie was twelve, Little King was seven, and Minnie was four years old. King's sister, Mandy, was living with them as well. It is interesting to note from the census that there were a number of other Turpin families whose properties were adjacent or near to King's at this time: Ephraim and Sallie Turpin; Martin and Julia Turpin; and Marian and Alice Turpin.[39]

---

[38] John Beatty, The Citizen-Soldier; or, Memoirs of a Volunteer, April 20, 1862, http:// www.perseus.tufts.edu/ hopper /text? doc= Perseus: text: 2001.05.0005: chapter%3D11.

[39] "1910 United States Federal Census, Roane County, Tennessee," Ancestry.com, http:// www.ancestry.com (accessed November 11, 2010).

There in Roane County, Minnie met Joshua King Christenberry's widow, Annie Christenberry. Here the story flashes back to 1872: Joshua King Christenberry seducing Minnie's grandmother, Serelda Turpin. Minnie's encounter with Annie Christenberry on this day suggests that the shame brought on by Serelda's affair with Mr. Christenberry in 1872 may have been lifted.

Aunt Mandy, who once had a reputation for being just as promiscuous as Serelda, took Minnie to the Christenberry house. Annie was very nice to Minnie. Annie took Minnie to a long table with a nice white table cloth. There Annie served her some milk, but Minnie spilled it. Annie responded, "Honey, I know you couldn't help it."[40]

Forty years earlier, the reputation of both families had been tainted. Somewhere between the lines may be a story of mercy, forgiveness and healing yet to be told.

Mischief and Discipline

In Minnie's opinion, she and Little King were "pretty mean kids." On one occasion, Little King set the wall-paper in the house on fire. The house almost burned down, but they managed to put it out.

Punishment was sometimes severe for such stunts. In an interview with Minnie, she reported that their father used to go after Little King with a hot poker, bricks or whatever was

---

[40] Interview with Minnie Belle Turpin Hall, about 1981.

handy. Their father had the reputation of being a short-tempered man.[41]

To illustrate King, Sr.'s short temper, someone has noted that on one occasion one of his sisters, Rosie, was baking bread; she was helping him keep house. She put too much baking powder in the dough mixture, and the bread did not come out right. What did King do? He ran Rosie out of the house.

King Remarries

As previously noted, for one to five years after Belle's death, King had no wife. When he did remarry, he married a seventeen year old girl named Annie. Her full name was Anna Elizabeth Lawson. King and Annie were married on June 3, 1911 in Roane County, Tennessee.[42] Minnie describes Annie as having red hair and fair skin.[43]

The children had no respect for their new step-mother. In Minnie's words, "She was just a kid herself." Annie used to lie down to read a lot, and the children would stick pins in her cushions so that she would be pricked by them. One time Minnie put a frog down her back, and on several occasions she put cow manure in the hen nests too. When

---

[41] Ibid.

[42] "Tennessee State Marriages, 1780-2002," Ancestry.com, http://www.ancestry.com (accessed November 11, 2010).

[43] Interview with Minnie Belle Turpin Hall, about 1981.

Annie went out into the barn to get the eggs, she reached up to get the eggs and stuck her hand in it!

Eventually Annie got involved with a black man and committed a crime for which she had to serve a year in prison. Minnie remembers Aunt Mandy taking her down to the courthouse for the trial in Kingston. After the sentence was pronounced, Annie said to Mandy, "Aunt Mandy, I have to go to jail."

Amanda replied, "Well, I thought you said that was your home." She had apparently been in there before. At that point, King proceeded to divorce her.[44]

A Move to Hardin Valley

The precise time of King's move from Roane County to Hardin Valley in Knox County is not yet known. While living in Hardin Valley, he gave Minnie a gift which once belonged to her mother. Minnie was big enough now, so her father gave her some side combs which Belle had worn in her hair. Minnie thought that was something great, but Little King took the combs, put them in the fire and burned them.

When their father got home, he asked Minnie, "Where are your mama's combs?"

She answered, "Brother burned them."

Little King said, "No, I didn't! You burned them!"

---

[44] Ibid.

Minnie insisted, "No, I didn't! You burned them!" They argued over it.

Finally their father said, "Well, I don't know which one of you burned them, so I'll whip you both, and that will get the right one!"

So, King whipped both of them.

Their father had gotten each of them a pair of shoes for Christmas. They would go to bed with them. Those shoes had to last them until the next Christmas, and if the shoes wore out, they would have to go bare-footed or wear rags or whatever they could get.

After King had whipped his children over the burning of the hair combs, he took their shoes away from them. He put them up and said, "When you can learn to behave yourselves, I'll give you your shoes."

When Sunday came, he would give them their shoes to go to church. After they returned home from church, he would put their shoes away again.[45]

Staying with Aunt Laura and Uncle Frank

Little King and Minnie often stayed with Aunt Laura and Uncle Frank for extended periods while their father was off working various jobs. Laura and Frank's small farm was a tranquil place, yet there was seldom an idle moment.

---

[45] Ibid.

Frank and Laura were hard working people. The corn that they raised was their main source of income. Often when visitors would come onto their property looking for them, they would find Aunt Laura and Uncle Frank praying and working in the fields at the same time.

In 2008 the author had the opportunity to walk the grounds of this old home place. The house featured a cistern from which water was drawn using a bucket secured by a rope. Frank had added at least one room, allowing a place for others to stay from time to time. Behind and beside the house were fields in which corn and other crops were grown. A small amount of livestock was raised as well.

About fifty yards to the north of the house was a barn. Beyond the barn, the land began to slope downward toward the spring at the edge of Beaver Creek. Walking the path toward the spring, one would first come to a small apple orchard. From there the path continued through the woods until the slope suddenly became very steep. The walk down to the spring was more like a downward climb. With Little King being required to bear part of the responsibilities of the farm while staying there, it is almost certain that he would have been familiar with the task of climbing up from that spring to carry water the distance of four hundred yards back to the house.

Going to Church

King had a difficult time raising the children alone, and he did not always treat them as he should have. According to Minnie, he wanted folks to think that he was a religious man, so he would sit and read the Bible to try to make that kind of impression. At night he would have Little King hold the candle for him to read, and if He didn't hold the light just right, he would spit tobacco juice in Little King's eye.

Although King's personal devotion to Christ seemed somewhat weak or even non-existent, he tried to keep Little King and Minnie in church. He took them to the holiness church—Providence Church of God where Uncle Frank and Aunt Laura attended in Solway.[46]

By this time, the Pentecostal experience to which Laura and Frank had been introduced at Chandlers View Baptist Church had become normative to the life of the worshipers who gathered at Providence Church of God—the church that would one day become known as Solway Church of God. The Providence church was located only two-hundred yards from the site where the Chandlers View congregants once worshiped.

What did Little King and Minnie see and experience while going to church with Frank and Laura? Obviously they would have witnessed the typical characteristics of Pentecostal worship—lively worship, anointed preaching,

---

[46] Ibid.

altar calls and manifestations of the Holy Ghost, but they also witnessed first-hand the personal devotion of their uncle and aunt.

Laura and Frank would leave home for the Sunday evening service at about 4:00 p.m.; the service started at 7:00 p.m. Departing from their house, they would cross Beaver Creek by walking across the Couch Mill dam. At other times, they would cross the field from their house there on the edge of Hardin Valley, walk about a mile down Steele Road, ford Beaver Creek or take a boat across when the water was up (later a swinging foot bridge was added). Laura would call out to a little boy named Truman Raby and ask him to come across with a boat to get them.[47] From there they would walk about a mile down Swafford Road, take a turn onto Guinn Road and finally end up on Solway Road where the church is located. Little King and Minnie would have been familiar with this four-mile walk to church.

In years to come, what would others remember about the spirituality of Frank and Laura? A number of people who knew them reported that many times when the Holy Ghost would come upon Laura, she would start walking the church floor swinging her hands. Her experience with God affected every facet of her worship as well as her daily life.

Charlotte Hinshaw adds,

> She was a blessed Saint of God. I can see her walking up and down the aisle of the church clapping her hands

---

[47] Interview with Daron Long.

ever so gently and just saying, "Woo! Woo! Woo!" As she would pass by you, the power of God could be felt coming from her.[48]

Frank had brown eyes and brown hair.[49] His hair was cut short, but it would not lie down on top. His hair would stick up like it often does on men when they get a crew cut. He wore clod hopper shoes and overhauls to church, and he often wore a red flannel shirt.[50]

When the power of God would come upon Frank, he would spin and dance in circles and make a sound like a freight train. Was the power of God really on Frank, or was he just getting emotionally worked up? If there were any doubts in anyone's mind, those doubts would have been removed whenever Frank shouted his way over to the red-hot pot-belly stove, lay his hands on it and not get burned. The people of the church felt that they always had good church services when Frank and Laura were there.[51]

Laura would often visit the sick and go from house to house inviting people to church. For years to come long-time residents of the valley would recall seeing the light of

---

[48] Interview with Charolette Hinshaw, 2009.

[49] "World War I Draft Registration Cards, 1917-1918, Record for Frank Turpin," Ancestry.com, http://www.ancestry.com (accessed November 16, 2010).

[50] Based on interviews with Barbara Hendrix, Rose Crawford, Katherine Nauman, and Grace Bowls.

[51] Ibid.

Laura's lantern at night, knowing that she was doing the work of the Lord.

Home Alone

King, Sr. often took his children with him when he was working a job, but after he moved his family to Hardin Valley, he had to leave his children at home alone over long periods of time. He would be gone for days at a time, finding whatever work he could—painting houses, doing farm work or repairing clocks and guns.[52]

With their father gone, the children did the best that they could to take care of themselves. Little King did the cooking. A lot of times he just fixed bread and water. In Minnie's own words,

> We were living by ourselves, I guess, probably half of the time. You might as well say that we pulled ourselves up. Of course, Daddy loved us, but he had to make a living. We had a pretty hard life.[53]

Going to School in Hardin Valley

Minnie continues with her memories of growing up and going to school in Hardin Valley:

> When I was growing up I had two dresses. I had one to wear to school, and when that dress was worn out, it was taken for everyday wear, and I would have one other

---

[52] Interview with Laura Turpin Dunaway, about 1980.
[53] Interview with Minnie Belle Turpin Hall, about 1981.

new one. Each of us had to do our own washing. We would go down to the river a lot of times and wash our clothes.[54]

In Hardin Valley the children had to walk about three miles to go to school. Little King and Minnie would carry their half-gallon lunch buckets in which their father had packed molasses and corn bread.

While walking through the fields on their way to school, they would pour out their food, go down into the gully and fill their buckets with slate rocks. They loved to eat slate rocks! Soon it became evident to King that something was wrong. In Minnie's words, "After awhile we got so pale we looked like dead children."

Their father followed them to school one day, saw them dumping their lunches and going down into the gully to get rocks.

"You talk about a whipping! We really got one," Minnie reports. They never picked up any more of those rocks.[55]

Dick and Lucy Steele

For some reason, neither Laura nor any other relatives were involved with the care of the children during this period of time. However, a neighboring couple, Dick and Lucy Steele, took special interest in the Turpin children and

---

[54] Ibid.
[55] Ibid.

frequently tended to them in their father's absence.[56] Dick was black, and Lucy was mulatto.[57]

On their way to school in Hardin Valley, Little King and Minnie would sometimes stop down on the branch to get duck eggs. They would take the eggs over to the store in Hardin Valley, sell them and buy brown sugar. For a dime they could get a pound of it. They ate a lot of brown sugar.

The ducks belonged to Dick Steele. He told Little King and Minnie that they could have all the eggs that they could find by the branch. The Steeles also gave the children milk.

Little King and Minnie went to pick peas for Dick and Lucy Steele one time. The Steeles saved part of the money out of the peas for the children and bought them clothes with it. They gave King the rest of the money. A lot of times Dick would stop his plowing, Lucy would prepare a dinner, and she would send Dick to the school to take the dinner to the Turpin children.

Minnie suffered from respiratory problems throughout her childhood. She remembered that people would not let her drink out of the dipper because they were afraid that she might spread the disease. She always wanted to be able to drink out of the dipper, but they served her water in a glass instead.

---

[56] Ibid.

[57] "1910 United States Federal Census, Knox County, Tennessee," Ancestry.com, http:// www.ancestry.com (accessed November 11, 2010).

Lucy Steele used to prepare a mixture of pine tar and honey and bring it over for Minnie. "Honey, you take that," Lucy would say. It was a sweet mixture. Minnie didn't mind taking it because it tasted so good.

King's remedy for Minnie's condition wasn't quite so pleasant. He would make her eat onions until she started "burning up," as Minnie put it. He would give her onions without bread or anything else to go with them. King would give Minnie anything that anybody recommended.

Lucy had dropsy,[58] and before she died she told her husband, "When I'm gone I want you to take them little Turpin kids what you don't want to keep of the canned stuff I've got." She had stored crocks of jam and jelly.

Shortly after Lucy died, her husband, Dick, fulfilled her request. He loaded up the wagon and brought a load of canned goods over to the Turpin house.[59]

Picking Strawberries

Every spring King took his children to the strawberry fields to pick berries. There were large patches of berries, and they were divided into rows. Long strings of people moved through the fields working the berry harvest. The elder King placed Minnie just ahead of him in his row and

---

[58] Dropsy is an old term referring to the swelling of soft tissue, often the result of what physicians today would call congestive heart failure.

[59] Interview with Minnie Belle Turpin Hall, about 1981.

let her pick the big berries and put them in her cup. He got the smaller berries behind her. Little King had a row to work by himself.

They picked from morning to night, and then they took their berries to a shed where they were deposited. Minnie carried a four quart container, and the others carried an eight quart container. They were paid one and a half cents per quart for their labor.[60]

Violence

Little King was about ten years old and Minnie was about eight (abt. 1913) when their father got entangled in a situation that led to violence.

While working the strawberry harvest, the elder King reportedly got involved with a woman that he had met there on the farm. One of the other laborers became jealous, and one day while King was out working in the berries, this man came after him and hit him in the head with a hoe.

That night a mob of men came to King's house and began to throw stones. King, Sr. pulled out the guns. He grabbed the shot gun, and he handed the pistol to Little King.

Both King and Little King stood beside the house and started shooting into the darkness until they heard a scream.

---

[60] Ibid.

The commotion stopped, and the mob scattered. After sunrise both father and son went outside to look things over. They found a hat soaked in blood with a bullet hole in it. No one ever reported whether or not a serious injury had occurred, and the mob never returned.

Apparently King occasionally carried a gun on other occasions. One day he was walking down a Knoxville street and saw a black man pushing people off of the sidewalk. He pushed King off too, but in defense, King drew his gun, shot the man and killed him on the spot. No charges were brought against him.[61]

A Move to Mullens Cove

It seems that King made a number of moves back and forth between the greater Knoxville area and the greater Chattanooga area. About twenty-five miles downstream from Chattanooga on the Tennessee River is a secluded place on a bend in the river called Mullens Cove. At some point between Belle's death and 1915, King moved to a place at or near Mullens Cove with Little King and Minnie. According to Minnie, their home was below the lock and dam.[62] However, Mullens Cove is located upstream from where the lock and dam stood at that time. This discrepancy in the story has not yet been resolved.

---

[61] Ibid.

[62] Interview with Minnie Belle Turpin Hall, about 1981.

Hales Bar Lock and Dam in 1913

Runaways

While King was living at Mullens Cove, the neighbor's child who was about Minnie's size would come over to play, but he was continually running home crying accusing Minnie and Little King of picking on him. But they were not fighting the child; they just wanted a playmate. When their father received this report, he punished both of them with a whipping. However, Minnie and Little King insisted that they were innocent.

The whippings occurred over the same accusations every day when King came home from work. Finally, Little King told his father, "Now, I didn't fight that kid!"

Minnie and Little King decided that if they got whipped over the lies of that child again, they would just run away from home. The whippings continued, so they decided to leave.

Early one morning before their father awoke, they made their way out of the house, went to the river's edge, and Little King chopped down the small tree to which the boat was chained. Their father had hidden the boat paddle, so they got a couple of planks to use for paddling the boat.

Minnie and Little King got on board the boat and set out to cross to the other side of the river. However, the water was rough, and white caps were forming. The waves were so high that the two children couldn't even see the banks of the river. They thought that they were going to die, so they kissed each other good-by.

However, the boat did make it to the opposite shore. The children managed to pull themselves off of the boat and onto the river bank, releasing the boat to the swift current and letting the river carry it away. Once they were safely on land, they climbed the bank and made their way toward a road.

Walking along the river, they stopped at homes to beg food. Actually, Little King made Minnie go up to the houses and ask for something to eat while he stood back. By his own admission, he was too ashamed to beg himself.

For three or four days, Little King and Minnie wandered from place to place until they found themselves in Chattanooga. Once they arrived in Chattanooga, they looked up a wealthy friend of the family—Captain Samuel Joseph Abner Frazier. The Turpins simply knew him as "Captain Frazier."

Captain S. J. A. Frazier

In Minnie Belle's words,

Captain Frazier was an old rich gentleman. He had a large house with servants and everything. He had served as a captain in the army, and one of his sons was a lawyer.[63]

Captain Frazier was a former Confederate captain. After the Civil War, he moved to Chattanooga, purchased a large tract of land across the river at the old Cowart farm and eventually began to lay out the Hill City suburb. The Fraziers moved into the old Cowart place, and the street that ran in front of the house, Frazier Avenue, was named after him.[64]

When Little King and Minnie arrived at Captain Frazier's house—an elegant home known at that time as "The Cedars"—they pretended that their father was in town and that he had sent them to Captain Frazier for a visit.[65]

---

[63] Interview with Minnie Belle Turpin Hall, abt. 1981.
[64] "Fraziers Date Back to City's Earliest Days," The Chattanoogan.com, http:// www.chattanoogan.com/ articles/ article_21797.asp (accessed November 17, 2010).
[65] The house was destroyed by a fire on March 13, 1923. Ibid.

Captain Frazier, his wife, Annie, and his daughter, Sarah Ruth Frazier,[66] warmly received Little King and Minnie and were good to them. He had a reputation in the city for being benevolent toward the poor.[67] The captain gave Minnie nickels and dimes just to rub his back.

Captain Frazier's daughter, Sarah Ruth Frazier

After several days of searching for his children, King Turpin lost hope and concluded that Minnie and Little King had drowned in the river. Hope returned, however, when people on the other side of the river began to report that they had seen two children begging for food and heading toward Chattanooga. With this promising lead,

---

[66] Sarah was later elected to the Tennessee State House of Representatives and served in that position from 1927 to 1929.

[67] Captain Frazier "had comprehensive knowledge of Latin and Greek and possessed a brilliant mind. He was an eloquent speaker and versatile writer and he stood as a splendid type of American manhood. The poor and needy and all who required assistance found him generous, kindly and benevolent. He was thoroughly modest, however, and was honest, upright and true in every relation of life. He commanded the highest respect and confidence of all who knew him." *Tennessee the Volunteer State 1769-1923: Volume 2*, Cited in "Descendants of George Thomas Frazier," Family Tree Maker, http:// familytreemaker.genealogy.com/ users/ f/ r/ a/ Donell-R-Frazier/ FILE/ 0002text.txt (accessed November 17, 2010).

King wrote a letter to Captain Frazier to see if the children might be at his house. [68]

The Cedars – Courtesy Chattanooga-Hamilton County Bicentennial Library

The two children feared what their father might do when they learned that he was coming to get them. However, instead of wrath, they were overwhelmed with their father's joy at seeing them alive.

---

[68] Captain Frazier died December 11, 1921 and is buried in the Confederate Cemetery near the campus of Tennessee University in Chattanooga. Much of the information contained in this chapter regarding Captain Frazier can be verified through numerous sources, including the local history files at the Chattanooga-Hamilton County Bicentennial Library.

When they returned to their home at Mullens Cove, King went over to the neighbor's house and told them that his children had been falsely accused. He said, "My children have not been fighting your kid! I'm not going to whip my children any more for things they have not done."

From that point forward, King tried to be more careful about passing judgment on Little King and Minnie.

Earthquake

On March 28, 1913, a strong earthquake shock centered at Knoxville was felt over an area of 7,000 square kilometers in East Tennessee.

> Two shocks were felt in many places. Movable objects were overthrown, and bricks fell from chimneys. A number of false alarms were set off at fire stations. Buildings throughout the city shook violently. The Knox County Courthouse, a massive brick structure, trembled noticeably. People outdoors experienced a distinct rise and fall in the ground; there were some cases of nausea.[69]

Although there are no known family stories related to the earthquake, it can be reasonably assumed that it might have been an event of concern to members of the family who were still living in the Knoxville area. It is unclear as to whether or not King and his children were in the area at this time.

---

[69] "Tennessee Earthquake History," USGS: Science for a Changing World, http:// earthquake.usgs.gov/ earthquakes/ states/ tennessee/ history.php (accessed November 11, 2010).

Back to Chattanooga

The story that follows suggests that King, Little King and Minnie were living back in Chattanooga in 1915-1916. In this period, state or local authorities intervened in Little King and Minnie's living situation.

Taken from their Father

Minnie's suffering from respiratory problems continued throughout her childhood, but her father would not take her in for proper medical treatment. State authorities finally determined that these children were being seriously neglected, so one day while their father was away, they came and took Minnie and Little King out of this situation. Minnie was picked up at home where she was sick in bed, and Little King was picked up at school.

Minnie ended up in Mother Reeves' children's home on Vine Street in Chattanooga, and on January 11, 1916, Little King went to Bonny Oaks boys home, also located in Chattanooga.[70] They took Little King to Bonny Oaks because he was a little too old for the orphanage on Vine Street.

When the authorities picked up Minnie, she told them that she was eighteen, and Little King told them that he was nineteen. In reality, Little King was about twelve years old. The Bonny Oaks school records show that he was fifteen

---

[70] On Google Earth, the central house of the Bonny Oaks home and school is located at latitude 35° 4'19.96"N, longitude 85°10'59.98"W.

years old. The children lied about their ages because they thought that they wouldn't have to stay there long if the authorities thought that they were older. Little King also told them that his name was "Bud."[71]

About this time, King, Sr. had a friend who had relatives in Rossville, Georgia, and this friend invited him to come with him on a visit to his family. During this visit, King met Ida Belle Conatser, the eighteen year old daughter of George and Sarah Hall Conatser, and they started courting.[72] King was forty-four years old.

On May 6, 1916, Bonny Oaks dismissed Little King and released him to his father who was at that time residing in North Chattanooga. However, Little King was released only with the understanding that he would be sent to Concord (or Hardin Valley) where his Uncle Frank would take care of him during minority.[73] Eight days later on May 14, 1916, King married Ida Belle Conatser in Walker County, Georgia. A Justice of the Peace named D. H. Hixon officiated.[74]

It took a little longer for Minnie to be released. Minnie remembers being in the orphanage for about two years

---

[71] Interview with Minnie Belle Turpin Hall, about 1981.

[72] Interview with Ida Belle Conatser Turpin, about 1981.

[73] This account has been verified via documentation provided by Bonny Oaks School, Chattanooga, Tennessee.

[74] Walker County, Georgia Vital Records: Marriages.

before Aunt Mandy came to get her. Most of her time at the orphanage had been spent in the hospital.[75]

Return to Hardin Valley

Immediately after King and Ida married, they lived in an apartment in Chattanooga—presumably North Chattanooga. Later they went back north to Hardin Valley where they moved in with Frank, Laura and Serelda to stay for awhile. It was at this point that King and his son, Little King, were reunited.

More Mischief

Little King stayed with King and Ida until he got married. Ida remembers him as being a hard worker; he helped them on the farm a lot.[76] However, as more stories begin to unfold, one can see that Little King still had a streak of mischief.

One day King sent Little King out to plant a field of corn. Little King planted until he got tired, and then he poured the rest of the seed into one hole and buried it. He slept the rest of the day. When he went back home his father asked him if he planted all of the corn. Little King answered, "Yes." Of course, when the corn finally came up he was in trouble.

---

[75] Interview with Minnie Belle Turpin Hall, about 1981.
[76] Interview with Ida Belle Conatser Turpin, about 1981.

On another occasion, Little King took off hunting, and King got mad at him because he wanted him to do some work in the corn field. When Little King came back, his father took the gun away from him. While King was talking to him, Little King threw a lantern at his father and then started running. The elder King got mad, took the gun and shot in the air toward his son. He didn't hit Little King; he was just trying to scare him.[77]

King told Little King to start the fire and keep it going in the wood stove one cold night. Instead of starting the fire, Little King lit a lantern and placed it inside the stove instead. From her place in bed, Ida could look out the bedroom door and see the stove. The glow of the lantern light gave the appearance that a fire was burning in the stove. However, when she and King noticed that the house wasn't getting any warmer, they became suspicious. When they checked the stove, they discovered Little King's deed.[78]

World War I

On April 6, 1917, the United States declared war on Germany and thus entered what was then known as the World War. It was also called the Great War or the War to End All Wars. Of course, it was not until the Second World War that it became known as World War I.

---

[77] Interview with Minnie Belle Turpin Hall, about 1981.
[78] Ibid.

In 1918 a wartime song entitled, "Long Boy," was released that Little King learned to sing and play on the guitar. Years later he would sing this song to his children and grandchildren:

Long Boy
By William Herschell and Barclay Walker

Good-bye, Ma!
Good-bye, Pa!
Good-bye, mule,
With your old hee-haw!
I may not know
What the war's about,
But you bet, by gosh,
I'll soon find out.

Whenever Little King sang this song as an adult, he left out the words "by gosh." He closed the song with "But you bet I'll soon find out."

King and Ida's First Son

In 1917, Little King gained a brother. On October 15, 1917, King and Ida's first son was born. They named him John Wesley Turpin.[79]

---

[79] "1920 United States Federal Census, Knox County, Tennessee," Ancestry.com, http://www.ancestry.com (accessed November 11, 2010). After King Sr.'s death, John ("Johnny") went to the CCC (Civilian Conservation Corps) camps when he was about 16 in Tiptonville, Tennessee. (The CCC was created under Roosevelt's

Minnie Returns Home

In time, King and Ida sent a letter to the orphanage in Chattanooga requesting that Minnie be released and be sent back to them. Arrangements were made, and Aunt Mandy went down to get Minnie and brought her back home. Minnie was twelve or thirteen years old at the time, according to her own report.[80]

Minnie Marries

When Minnie was about thirteen years old she married a man named Lawrence Freels, became pregnant by him and was then abandoned by him.[81] At that point she went to stay with Henry Wright and his wife up in the mountains. They tried to pass her off as their daughter for some reason. That family was mean to her, so she tried to run off. She tried to write to her father several times, but her letters were always returned to Henry by the postman.

New Deal. It provided employment for about three million young men. Their work included forestry, fire fighting, flood control, and swamp drainage. The recruits were required to send home most of their pay.) He was there at the time of the flood at about 1933. John Wesley got malaria fever and almost died. He came back to the Knoxville area. After he was too old for the CCC camps, he joined the army (World War II). Johnny took part in Lt. General Montgomery's successful pursuit of Rommel (November 8, 1942 - May 13, 1943) and died in combat in North Africa on May 23, 1943.
[80] Interview with Minnie Belle Turpin Hall, about 1981.
[81] It is assumed that this baby was either lost by miscarriage or that it died in infancy.

Finally, Minnie was able to run off. She went over a mountain and came to a road and started picking strawberries to eat because by this time she was hungry. Eventually she came to the house of a man named Chet Watson and knocked on his door. She did not tell him that she was a runaway. She just said that she wanted some work picking strawberries.

Chet asked, "Where is your luggage?"

"I don't have any," replied Minnie.

The Watsons felt sorry for her, so they told her that she could use one of the rooms above the garage. Mrs. Watson went to the store and got materials to make Minnie some clothes. They told Minnie that as she worked picking strawberries, she could pay them back for whatever it cost to make the dresses. Mrs. Watson also gave Minnie some dresses that one of her daughters had outgrown.

Three days passed, and Minnie was out in the field working. There was a knock at the Watson door. It was Henry Wright.

"Have you seen a girl by the name of Minnie Freels?" Henry asked.

Chet replied, "I haven't ever heard of that girl."

"Well, maybe she went by her maiden name--Minnie Turpin," Henry said.

At that point Chet knew who Henry was talking about. "A girl came by here a few days ago by that name, and she is working for me now."

Chet then took Henry Wright out into the fields to where Minnie was picking strawberries. Mr. Wright approached Minnie and ordered, "Come on Minnie, we're going home! Mandy wants you to come back and live with us."

"I'm not going back!" Minnie responded.

Mr. Wright bent over, picked up a root and insisted, "You're coming back! If you don't come back, I'm going to kill you!"

Minnie answered, "Well, go ahead and kill me! I'd rather be dead than to go back!"

Chet Watson spoke up, "If she wants to, she can go with you, but if she doesn't want to go, she doesn't have to."

Henry got angry. Chet ordered him off of his property, "I've heard about you! You've got a bad reputation around here! I'm ordering you off of my land!" By that time there were a lot of hired hands gathered around. Henry Wright was outnumbered. He left.

Chet then turned to Minnie and asked, "Your name is Minnie Turpin?"

"Yes," Minnie answered.

"Are you King Turpin's daughter?" Chet asked.

"Yes!" Minnie said with excitement as she realized that Chet knew something about her family.

With a smile Chet said, "Did you know that I showed you how to pick your first strawberries with your father?"

A little while later, King and Little King came in Little King's car to get Minnie and take her home. Minnie would soon marry a man named Joe Raby, and after his death she would marry Joe Hall. In Minnie's own words, "I had two good husbands."[82]

The Family Grows and Moves

Ida Belle Conatser Turpin

In the early 1920's, King and Ida's family continued to grow. About 1920 a daughter named Grace was born, and about 1921 Ida gave birth to another daughter that they named Georgia L. Turpin.[83]

Eventually King, Ida and the children got a house of their own and moved out of Frank and Laura's place. On August 22, 1923, King purchased 12½ acres in Hardin Valley from Amanda Stubbs for the purchase price of "one dollar and love and affection."[84]

---

[82] Interview with Minnie Belle Turpin Hall, about 1981.
[83] 1930 Census of Knox County, Tennessee.

According to Ida, when she and King lived in Hardin Valley, he had a camera with which he took their picture in front of the dresser mirror. She never did know what happened to that picture. As a matter of fact, she is not even sure that it was ever developed. That photo may have been the only picture ever taken of King.[85]

Two Kings on a Motorcycle

Little King used to take his father's motorcycle and ride it without permission, but one day his father was riding on the back while he was driving. They climbed to the top of a hill, and when they stopped Little King said, "We really climbed up that hill that time, didn't we Dad!"

He turned around, and his father wasn't there! He had fallen off somewhere along the way.[86]

Little King Enters Adulthood

At this point in his life, Little King was probably no longer addressed by the name "Little King." However, for those years of this narrative that still involve his father, the

---

[84] Registry of Deeds at the East Tennessee History Center, Knoxville, TN (Book 382, Page 257). Amanda's husband was William N. Stubbs.

[85] Interview with Ida Belle Conatser Turpin, about 1981.

[86] This account is based on a synthesis of the story as King's children remember him telling it and the author's Interview with Minnie Belle Turpin Hall, about 1981.

name "Little King" will still be used to help the reader distinguish between the two men.

Little King's sister, Minnie, married a man named Joe Raby. Shortly after their marriage, Little King started dating Joe Raby's sister. However, on their first date, she did nothing but giggle. Little King just walked away and left her. He thought that she was acting too silly. She started calling out, "I'm going to have him yet!"

In the words of Bertha Church, who married Little King a few years later: "She never got him."[87]

Some have noted other interesting facts about King's young adult years. Reportedly he was a member of the Tennessee militia. He also belonged to a secret society where he had a secret name.[88]

Prophetic Encounter

Throughout Little King's childhood and teenage years, he had been repeatedly exposed to the truth of the Gospel through the influence of Aunt Laura, Uncle Frank and Providence Church of God. Now that he had entered adulthood, he still had not embraced the grace he had been offered. In fact, years later when King, Jr. reflected back on these years, he stated that he was an infidel prior to becoming a Christian.

---

[87] Interview with Bertha Lee Church Turpin/Green.
[88] Jim Turpin, Interview with family members, 2010.

Just a few years prior to his conversion, he was either visiting or staying at his Aunt Laura's house. She had a minister come in. The Holy Ghost spoke through that man and told Little King about his life. This man did not know Little King, and he knew nothing about him. He told him things about himself that only God knew. That prophetic encounter made an impression on Little King that would bear fruit later.[89]

Little King Marries

At the age of eighteen, Little King was employed at a cotton mill in Knoxville, Tennessee. While working there, he met a young woman named Nellie Griggs, daughter of Merritt Henry Griggs[90] and Margaret Hettie Brown. On August 12, 1921, Little King and Nellie got married.[91]

To place the time of King and Nellie's marriage in historical context, 1921 was also the year that Warren G. Harding was inaugurated as President, and the United States formerly ended World War I.

For a time King and Nellie lived in Lovell, Tennessee--an area west of the city of Knoxville.[92] Lovell was not far from the site of Campbell Station—the vicinity where some

---

[89] Jim Turpin, Interview with Alice Turpin Hatfield, May 2010.

[90] First and middle names of Mr. Griggs, source: Carolyn Griggs Moore (Email received March 21, 2010). Nellie's death record shows that her father's last name was McGrigger.

[91] The marriage record shows Nellie's maiden name as Greigg.

[92] Certificate of Death, Agnes Pearl Turpin.

believe Martin Turpin might have lived when he arrived in Tennessee between 1797 and 1805.

Nellie Griggs Turpin. Photo provided by Carolyn Griggs Moore.

The Birth of Pearl Turpin

When King was nineteen years old, he and Nellie had their first child. Agnes Pearl Turpin was born on July 30, 1922 in Lovell.[93] They called her Pearl. Another Turpin generation had begun, but little did King and Nellie know the sorrow that awaited them in the next chapter of their journey together.

Departure from the Tennessee River Valley

For over one hundred twenty years, the Turpins had lived along the Tennessee River. With the start of the next

---

[93] Ibid.

chapter, Little King would depart from this familiar valley and set out northward with Nellie and Pearl to start a new life in the mountains of Kentucky—far away from parents and siblings. From this point forward in the narrative, he will no longer be referenced as Little King. Hereafter he will be called King or King, Jr.

Chapter 2

Life in Kentucky

In the 1920's, U.S. Coal & Coke owned the world's largest coal tipple with a capacity of 15,000 tons. It was located in Lynch, Kentucky (Harlan County). On February 12, 1923 the world's record for coal production in a single nine hour shift was achieved when miners operating forty shortwall cutting machines produced 12,820 tons of coal, filling 256 railcars.[94]

Tipple located in Lynch, Kentucky

[94] "History of Portal 31," Portal 31: Kentucky's First Exhibition Coal Mine, http:// www.portal31.org/ history_of_portal_31.htm (accessed November 11, 2010).

King, Nellie and their baby, Pearl, moved to Lynch, Kentucky where King began his work as a coal miner. This move took place at some point between July 30, 1922 (the date of their daughter's birth in Lovell, Tennessee) and August 7, 1923 (the date that the doctor in Kentucky last saw their daughter alive).[95]

Pearl's Death

Shortly after King and Nellie moved to Kentucky, Pearl died. She was one year old. According to oral history, she died from accidentally swallowing some carbide--the chemical substance that miners used to light the lamps which they wore on their hats. Her death certificate shows that she died from acute enterocolitis. She died on August 8, 1923.[96]

Beginning to Pray

It is believed that in the midst of these days of sorrow, King began to pray. He had not yet come to a point of personal conversion to faith in Christ, but because of Aunt Laura's influence, he did know when to call on the Lord in times of need.

The dangers of King's new vocation presented reason enough to pray. Working in a cotton mill in Knoxville was

---

[95] Certificate of Death, Agnes Pearl Turpin.
[96] "Kentucky Death Records, 1852-1953," Ancestry.com, http:// www.ancestry.com (accessed November 11, 2010).

one thing, but descending every day into the bowels of the earth to mine coal was a different matter altogether. King was very much aware of the fact that on any given day there was the possibility that he might not return to the surface alive. He prayed. He called upon the Lord. His heart was nearly ready for what was yet to come.

The Birth of Jack Turpin

At the time of Pearl's death, Nellie was already pregnant bearing a second child. On February 6, 1924, King and Nellie's second child was born in Lynch. They named him James Jackson Turpin; he would be known by the name, Jack.[97] To place Jack's birth in historical context, 1924 is also the year that United States citizenship was granted to all Native Americans; Calvin Coolidge was elected as President; and the first Macy's Thanksgiving Day Parade was held in New York City.

The Birth and Death of Robert Turpin

Robert Turpin was born to King and Nellie on October 27, 1925 in Lynch. They called him Bob. (Another son by the name of Robert would be born to King and his second wife, Bertha, a few years later.) In May of 1927, the child was

---

[97] "Kentucky Birth Index, 1911-1999, James J. Turpin" Ancestry.com, http://www.ancestry.com (accessed November 16, 2010). Some have said that his middle name was Jackson and not Jack. In this book, his name may appear both ways in various places.

overtaken with pneumonia. He was under a doctor's treatment from May 1 to May 22. Robert died on May 22, 1927 in Lynch and was buried the same day in Cumberland, Kentucky. The death certificate shows that during this time the family lived at #928 Lynch, Kentucky.[98]

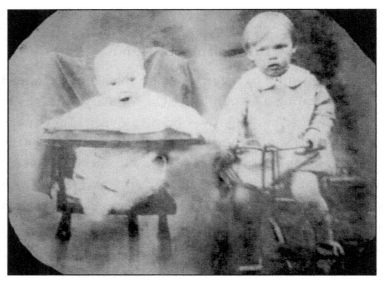

**The child on the left is Robert and the child on the right is Jack.
(Source: Darlene Turpin Feathers)**

Sorrow Back Home

Between the time of Robert's birth and the date of his death, back home in Tennessee two family members were approaching their final days. It is not known whether or not King and Nellie were aware of what was transpiring at the

---

[98] Certificate of Death, Robert Turpin.

time. King's grandmother, Serelda, died at the age of 75 on September 27, 1926 at 6:10 p.m. at Frank and Laura's house in Hardin Valley.[99]

According to Dr. A. R. Garrison, Serelda died of cancer which had overtaken her nose and the right side of her face. He last saw her alive seven days earlier, on September 20th. She was buried two days after her death in the Providence Church of God Cemetery in Solway. Her name on the tombstone is displayed as "Rildia Turpin." The death certificate was signed by Laura's son, Sherman Dunaway.[100] According to Laura's report years later, her mother died having never come to a point of personal faith in Christ.[101]

Exactly one month later, Serelda's sister, Amanda, died of a heart attack and stroke in the same house. In her final moments, she suddenly spun around and around in the floor. They managed to get her to bed, but within a short time she was dead. She was 78 years old. Amanda was buried beside her sister, Serelda.

In the midst of all of this loss, however, King and Ida were celebrating another birth. In 1926 another son, Albert D. Turpin, was born.[102]

---

[99] Certificate of Death, Serelda Turpin.

[100] Ibid.

[101] Interview with Laura Turpin Dunaway, about 1980.

[102] "1930 United States Federal Census, Knox County, Tennessee," Ancestry.com, http://www.ancestry.com (accessed November 11, 2010).

Salvation

What caused the heart of King, Jr. to turn? Was it the dangers of his vocation? Was it the tragic loss of two of his children? Was he wrestling with a sense of guilt—the feeling that he was at fault for Pearl's death? No doubt such circumstances had some bearing on his soul; however, the precise sequence of incidents and circumstances leading to King's conversion is not known.

It happened at a cottage prayer meeting in Lynch, Kentucky. King knelt down at a chair and received Jesus Christ as his Lord and Savior. When he stood to his feet, he heard a voice that said, "It's a comin'! It's a comin'! It's a comin'!"

At that moment the power of the Holy Ghost rushed from the top of his head down to his feet, and he began to speak in tongues.[103] It was probably about this same time that Nellie became a Christian. The seed that Aunt Laura had planted into a young life years earlier was bearing fruit.

When King was converted, the change became immediately obvious. No one had to tell him that he needed to stop smoking. No doubt, Aunt Laura's influence had something to do with it, but most certainly it was the conviction and power of the Holy Ghost that enabled him to quit instantly.

---

[103] Mark 16:7; Acts 2; 10:46; 19:6; 1 Corinthians 12-14.

King's Ministry Begins

It did not take long. King soon knew that God's call was upon his life, and he began to preach the Gospel message. His message had a three-fold emphasis: salvation, sanctification and the baptism in the Holy Ghost. He traveled to mountain communities with other men whom God had called. They played their musical instruments together; they sang, and they preached.

At times King met people who had absolutely no knowledge of Christianity. One day he asked a man if he knew that Jesus had died for his sins, and the man sincerely responded, "No, I didn't even know that He was sick!"

Among the miners in Lynch, King became known as a preacher. One day another miner grabbed him by the ear, started twisting it and began mocking him, saying, "Preach preacher man! Preach for me!"

In an instant, the power of God knocked the man about ten feet across the mine. King had not touched him.

The man was a former Swedish boxer. He told others what happened, warning them, "*Never* mess with that man!"

The man repented; his whole family turned their hearts to the Lord; and he became one of King's best friends. Being a former boxer, he later reported, "I have been hit hard before, but never like that."

The Birth and Death of Willie Turpin

Willie Turpin was born to King and Nellie in Kentucky sometime in 1927. However, on July 6, 1928, the baby died of gastro enteritis. He was one year old. According to the death certificate, he was buried in Cumberland, Kentucky the following day. The record shows that the family lived at #784 Lynch, Kentucky. In the handwriting of the physician, these words can be read on the death certificate: "The family never gave any medication; they believe in divine healing."[104]

Sadly, those recorded words comprise the first documented evidence that King had experienced a conversion to faith in Christ. It was not uncommon in those days for Pentecostal believers to refuse medical treatment, thinking that to accept treatment would be a denial of their faith in Christ as Healer. Later it is clear that King took a more moderate position on the relationship between divine healing and medical assistance.

In the same year that Willie died, back home in Tennessee, another son was born to King, Sr. and Ida— Daniel N. Turpin. King, Jr. did not maintain much contact with his Tennessee family; therefore, he may not have

---

[104] "Kentucky Death Records, 1852-1953," Ancestry.com, http://www.ancestry.com (accessed November 11, 2010).

known about his half-brother's birth.[105] Two years later in 1929, King, Sr., Ida and their children moved from Hardin Valley to Knoxville.

The Birth of Pauline Turpin

On January 3, 1929, King and Nellie's first daughter was born—Pauline Elizabeth Turpin. To place Pauline's birth in historical context, 1929 was the year that Herbert Hoover was inaugurated as the President of the United States. It was also the year that the stock market crashed. Shortly after Pauline's birth, the family began making plans for a move out West.

Bloody Harlan

Throughout the 1920s and well into the 1930s, the U.S. Coal & Coke company, along with many Kentucky coal producers, did everything in their power to prevent unionization. This action by the coal companies and the actions of the miners earned Harlan County the name of "Bloody Harlan."[106] A culture of violence was about to erupt in Harlan County. Providentially, King moved his family out of this region before the worst of it began.

---

[105] "1930 United States Federal Census, Knox County, Tennessee," Ancestry.com, http://www.ancestry.com (accessed November 11, 2010).

[106] "History of Portal 31," Portal 31: Kentucky's First Exhibition Coal Mine, http:// www.portal31.org/ history_of_portal_31.htm (accessed November 11, 2010).

Chapter 3

Life Out West

At some point between 1929 and 1930, King and Nellie packed up their T-Model Ford, departed from the mountains of Kentucky, and moved their family westward, leaving the coal mines of Kentucky behind them. They took Nellie's 67 year old mother, Margaret, with them.[107] The copper mines of Miami, Arizona (Gila County)—two thousand miles away—would be King's ultimate destination, but while en route he took time to minister in Arkansas. The details of King's ministry in Arkansas or in other places along the way are not known.

King's life had taken him from the river to the mountains. Now he was venturing from the mountains to the desert. The desert community of Miami, Arizona was located about thirty miles to the east of Phoenix. Although Miami had previously been known for its silver mines, by this time copper mining was booming. King had come to work as a laborer in the open-pit mines.

---

[107] "1930 United States Federal Census, Gila County, Arizona," Ancestry.com, http://www.ancestry.com (accessed November 11, 2010).

Miami, Arizona in 1920, about ten years before King's arrival

That T-Model Ford

When King arrived in Arizona, a neighbor told him he should not park his T-Model Ford in the location he had chosen. King moved his car and soon learned why his former parking place was such an issue. When the rain came, the place where he had previously parked became a river.

That T-Model Ford did not handle very well in the western states. It easily overheated in that climate. To remedy the problem, King installed a water pump and a fan with additional blades. The T-Model did not typically have a water pump. After King installed that water pump, he would often pass overheated cars along the road, but his car would just keep going.

King discovered an unusual use for that car. He found that a jack rabbit for dinner could be obtained by chasing it with the T-Model. When the car was over it, the rabbit would jump up, hit its head underneath, and the car would knock it out. At that point, all King had to do was stop the car, get out and finish the work.

Divine Protection

One day while working at the mine, King heard a man call out, "Fire in the hole!" signaling the workers to prepare for an imminent blast. But at the same time, King heard another voice—either the voice of God or an angel, shouting, "Jump!"

King jumped. While in the air, the force of the explosion knocked him over the bank; flying rock passed over him, and he was shielded from harm as he lay behind the bank. His life had been spared for God's own purpose.

Evangelistic Work

King evangelized while he was out West. Nellie served with him in the ministry of prayer in these settings. Although King was not credentialed with the Church of God, he did consider himself a Church of God minister at this time. King had grown up under the influence of the Church of God, a Pentecostal denomination, through his association with Aunt Laura and Uncle Frank.[108] Laura and Frank attended Providence Church of God in Solway, Tennessee.

King Turpin, Jr.
(About 1930-32)

On one occasion while preaching in an Assemblies of God, he gave a message through tongues and interpretation. Through the message, the Holy Ghost called for the congregation to be sanctified. According to the family's oral history, the impact of King's ministry was so significant that the church decided to affiliate with the Church of God.[109]

Supernatural Utterance

The gift of tongues and the gift of interpretation were frequently manifested in King's ministry.[110] In one church service, King spoke in tongues in one dialect, and then interpreted. He spoke again in a different dialect, and then interpreted. An ex-catholic priest stood and said,

---

[108] The international headquarters for the Church of God is located in Cleveland, Tennessee.

[109] Interview with James (Jim) Randolph Turpin, Sr., May 24, 2010.

[110] 1 Corinthians 12-14. Such charismatic gifts are commonly manifested among Pentecostal Christians.

This man has spoken in Spanish, and interpreted perfectly what he said. Then he spoke in Greek, and interpreted what he said. He has done it well.[111]

The priest could speak seven different languages.[112]

On one occasion a man was speaking in tongues, and King could not get the interpretation. Later King found out that the man was testing him. This fellow man was not really speaking in tongues; he was speaking out a grocery list in Polish. After the man realized that King could not be deceived, he confessed to his attempt at trickery.

In another service, King went to a church where there were a lot of Spanish-speaking people. He told the pastor that he would have to have an interpreter. However, when he got up to speak, the Holy Ghost moved upon him, and he preached in another language, which he soon realized was Spanish. When he was finished, many people had been touched. The interpreter said that he had delivered the sermon in fluent Spanish.[113]

Miraculous Healings

King traveled a lot evangelizing in various places. While driving to one speaking engagement, he and his family were involved in a car accident. Jack's back was broken.

---

[111] Jim Turpin, Interview with family members, May 2010.
[112] Ibid.
[113] Jim Turpin, Interview with Roger Turpin, May 2010.

Jack was taken to the hospital, and the doctors said that there was little that they could do for him. They said that Jack would not walk again. But King said, "Well, we are going to pray about this."

As soon as the doctor left, King said to Jack, "You will walk again. God will heal you."

He started praying. The Spirit of God moved upon Jack, and he was healed instantly.

"Son, let's go. We're leaving this place," King said.

Jack got up, put his clothes on, and they just left.[114]

This was not the only time that Jack experienced the power of God. On another occasion, he was playing on the rooftop and fell off. His collar bone was broken. King prayed for him, and God healed Jack instantly.[115]

Signs, Wonders and Burning Coals

Other signs and wonders accompanied King's ministry. In one worship service out West, he took off his coat, walked over to the red-hot pot-bellied stove at the side of the room and began to run his hands up and down the sides of it! In telling this story years later, with a sound of reverence and

---

[114] Ibid.

[115] Interview with James (Jim) Randolph Turpin, Sr., May 24, 2010. Years later—just a few months before Jack died—he recalled that incident of healing. While reflecting on God's merciful dealings with him over the years, in the presence of a number of his siblings, Jack prayed and received Christ as his Lord and Savior.

amazement in his voice he would say, "That stove felt smooth as velvet."

Then he opened the door with his bare hand, reached into the fire, scooped up some burning coals in his hands and held them out before the people without being burned. The fear of the Lord settled upon the assembly. King had no burns; not even a trace of soot or ashes were on his long-sleeved white shirt.[116]

An Available Servant

King lived his life as one who was available to serve the Lord in whatever way he might be needed. While in Arizona King came to the aid of an infant who had been stung by a scorpion. He rushed the child and his mother to the hospital in his car with his horn blowing. The doctor said that King saved the little girl's life. God had placed King at the right place at the right time to come the aid of a child in need.

Hispanic Influence

Living and working among Spanish-speaking people in the region helped King to acquire some knowledge of the language. Years later he would tease his grandchildren with various Spanish expressions. He would speak a few Spanish words and act like he was surprised that his grandchildren couldn't understand him. Then he would just laugh.

---

[116] According to Alice Turpin Hatfield, this same miracle occurred a second time years later at a church service in West Virginia.

The Birth of Virginia Turpin

Virginia Nell Turpin, daughter of King and Nellie, was born June 12, 1931 in Miami, Arizona.[117] To place her birth in historical context, 1931 was also the year that Thomas Edison submitted his last patent application; the *Star-Spangled Banner* was adopted as the United States' national anthem; the Empire State Building was completed in New York City; and the comic strip, *Dick Tracy*, made its debut.

Back East

After Virginia's birth, King began considering a move back East. King had a Hungarian friend who had been living in McDowell County, West Virginia since at least 1930.[118] His name was Charlie Gary--a fellow-minister of the Gospel. Charlie had encouraged King to move to Kimball, so one day—about 1932—the family loaded up in their Big Six Studebaker and took off for West Virginia.

---

[117] "Obituaries," Fostoria.org, http:// www.fostoria.org/ CalBits/ Obituaries/ archive/ 2000 /a_b.html#47 (accessed November 11, 2010).

[118] "1930 United States Federal Census, McDowell County, West," Ancestry.com, http://www.ancestry.com (accessed November 11, 2010).

Chapter 4

Life in West Virginia

Departing from Arizona, Little King, Nellie and the children set out on their two thousand mile journey back East. After driving seventeen hundred miles through New Mexico, Texas, Oklahoma and Arkansas, they stopped in Knoxville, Tennessee for a short visit before continuing on to West Virginia. Years later, King's sister, Minnie, would recall that she saw her brother in 1932. Nellie's mother, Margaret ("Grandma Griggs"), continued with them on their move to West Virginia.

At the time of King, Jr.'s visit, King, Sr. may have been working as a motion picture projectionist. He also continued to work on clocks and guns. In addition to seeing his father and step-mother, Ida, King, Jr. may have also spent time with some of his half-brothers and sisters who were at home--Johnnie, Grace, Georgia, Albert and Daniel.[119]

After driving a little over two hundred miles further northeast, King and his family finally arrived in McDowell County, West Virginia. Upon arriving in the town of

---

[119] "1930 United States Federal Census, Knox County, Tennessee," Ancestry.com, http:// www.ancestry.com (accessed November 11, 2010).

Kimball, King secured a job in the Carswell coal mine and moved his family in with Charlie and Bertha Gary.

King and Charlie started ministering together through music and the preaching of the Gospel in the surrounding communities. In addition to playing the guitar, King also played a six-stringed guitar-banjo.[120]

Bertha's parents,
William and Rebecca Church

One place where King held prayer meetings was the home of William Isaac Church on Rock House Mountain. (William's wife, Rebecca Workman Church, had died about four years earlier.) Nellie felt at home at the Church place, so the Turpins spent a lot of time there.

The Death of Nellie and Her Twins

Nellie was pregnant, and not long after the family's arrival in West Virginia, she went into premature labor.[121] The date was November 4, 1932. Cora Bennett, who was a

[120] In King's latter years he would purchase another guitar-banjo. Before he died, he asked that the instrument be passed on to his son, Jim. On November 17, 2009, Jim gave the guitar-banjo to his son—the author.

[121] Nellie's death record shows that the babies were born premature. Certificate of Death, Nellie Turpin.

mid-wife, came to assist, and Nellie gave birth to two babies—Edward and Edgar. However, the intensity of the event was not relieved by the successful delivery. Nellie's bleeding would not stop. Someone sent for Dr. Cochran, but there was no time; Nellie's life began to pass from her. As she was about to slip into eternity, she started speaking in tongues, and then she died. Nellie was twenty-nine years old.[122]

Dr. Cochran arrived about three hours after the babies had been born. Nellie had passed so quickly that there was no way that the doctor could have arrived in time to make any difference.

Years later, Pauline Turpin Davis reflected on Nellie's death. She recalled that her father, King, lifted her up to the coffin to see her mother one last time before they buried her.

After Nellie died, Grandma Griggs took care of the twins. However, she neglected them, and their health began to fail. Fifteen days after Nellie's death, on November 19, 1932, Edward died.[123] He was buried the next day— November 20th. Twenty-eight days after Nellie's death, on December 2, 1932, Edgar died.[124] He was buried the next

---

[122] Ibid.

[123] Edward Turpin's death record shows that the cause of his death was his premature birth. Certificate of Death, Edward Turpin.

[124] Edgar Turpin's death record shows that the cause of his death was "prematurity." Certificate of Death, Edgar Turpin.

day—December 3rd. Nellie and her two infant children are buried on Rock House Mountain.

William Church's house on Rock House Mountain

King Remarries

Within only a few days of Edgar's death, King approached William Church and asked for his daughter's hand in marriage. Her name was Bertha Lee Church.[125] Bertha had been helping to take care of King's children— Jack, Pauline and Virginia—after Nellie's death. On the day after Christmas, December 26, 1932, King and Bertha were married. Reverend J. W. Wooding performed the

---

[125] Bertha's parents were William Church and Rebecca Workman.

ceremony.[126] King and Bertha spent their wedding night camping out on the side of the hill by Bean Field Road on Rock House Mountain.

Several sources confirm that King gave William his Big Six Studebaker in exchange for Bertha. Bertha reports, "My dad traded me for the car. King said that if he hadn't given my Dad the car, he wouldn't have got me!"[127]

From 1932 to 1936, King managed to get around without a motorized vehicle. He also managed to work the farmland without the assistance of a horse or a mule. When King first got married to Bertha, he used to pull the plow himself to work the ground.

Bertha's Salvation

While Bertha was pregnant with her first child, she and King were staying with the Gary family. One night in a prayer meeting at Charlie Gary's house, she knelt beside her husband and received Jesus as her Lord and Savior. She remembers that it felt like a great weight was lifted off of her.

At a time when King was not present, Bertha received the baptism in the Holy Ghost. From that point forward, she

---

[126] "McDowell County, West Virginia Marriages," West Virginia Division of Culture and History, http:// www.wvculture.org/ vrr/ va_view.aspx?Id=11416843&Type=Marriage (accessed November 12, 2010).

[127] Interview with Bertha Lee Church Turpin/Green, May 2010.

served with her husband in ministry. They went to conduct church services together; King preached, Bertha spoke in tongues, and King interpreted the tongues. Later God gave Bertha the gift of interpretation as well. Bertha describes their ministry together:

> We would work together praying with people. We would go and sing, pray, give out messages, interpret. We would conduct prayer meetings, and people would get saved and sanctified.[128]

Whenever they visited people in their homes, they would never leave a person's house without praying.[129]

The Death of King's Father

Far away in Knoxville, Tennessee, on March 29, 1933 King's father, King Sr., died. In these latter years of King, Sr.'s life, he had suffered from a diseased liver. The doctor said that it was both incurable and fatal. However, the disease was not the cause of King's death. The account of his death originally posted on the author's blog site follows:

> King had set up a place in his house in Knoxville where he could work on watches, clocks and guns. When the house next door became available, he decided to move there because the lighting was better; there were not as many other houses blocking the sunlight, and more sunlight would make it easier for him to work.

---

[128] Ibid.

[129] Jim Turpin, Interview with Alice Turpin Hatfield, May 2010.

Everything had been moved over to the new house by hand, except for the piano which he had acquired for the girls to play. They went and got the pick-up truck and began loading the piano onto it.

"King, let's place the piano on its back," someone suggested. "No, let's keep it upright," King insisted.

So, they loaded the piano upright, pulled away from the porch of the house from which they were moving, and King walked alongside the truck. He had two boys on the back of the pick-up—one on each side holding the piano. When they started backing up to the door of their new home, one wheel of the truck ran up on a little bank. The piano started reeling and rocking.

As Ida watched from the front porch of the old house and all of the children and other family members were standing by, King ran to the back of the truck and got under the piano to hold it steady. When he saw that it was really going to fall, he stepped back, but when he stepped back he fell onto the hard ground beneath. Quickly he tried to get out of the way of it, raised his hands up like he was trying to hold it, and the piano suddenly turned a flip, and fell on its back on top of King, bounced a foot off of the ground after impact, and finally came to rest on top of him. It killed him right there.

The moment Minnie had seen what was about to happen, she jumped down from the porch where she was standing, thinking that she might be able to pull her father out of the way in time (King was just a little man weighing about 120 pounds, according to Minnie), but by the time her feet hit the ground, it was too late.

Quickly the men rushed to lift the heavy instrument off of him. In an instant others sprang forward to help.

As soon as King was uncovered, Minnie was there clutching at her Daddy's coat. She picked him up by the coat. Ida ran her arms under his head, but his head was mashed flat, and his body was broken open. In Ida's words, the piano had "mashed his insides out." Nothing could be done. Aunt Laura reports, "He just straightened out; he was gone. He didn't have any time."

In a panic, a few of them carried King's body into the house and put him on a bed.

When Aunt Laura shared her version of the story, she concluded by saying, "He didn't have any time. I tell you, if people ain't gonna get prepared when they're alive and when they can, they just miss everything.... They just miss it all."

At the time that King was killed, Ida was pregnant with Edna....[130]

By the time the news of his father's death reached Rock House Mountain (near Kimball, West Virginia), it was too late for King to go to the funeral. His father was buried in

---

[130] J. Randolph Turpin, Jr., "An Account of King Turpin's Death," Turpin Tree: Researching Turpin Family Origins, entry posted November 6, 2009, http://turpintree.blogspot.com/2009/11/account-of-king-turpins-death.html (accessed November 12, 2010).

the Providence Church of God cemetery in Solway. The epitaph on his tombstone reads, "Gone but not forgotten."

The Birth of Jim Turpin

Nearly one year after Nellie's death, on November 11, 1933, King and Bertha's first son was born at the Stevens Clinic Hospital in Welch. His full name was James ("Jim") Randolph Turpin. They called him "Jimmy."[131] At the time of Jimmy's birth, King and Bertha were still living with Bertha's father, William Church.

To place Jim's birth in historical context, 1933 was also the year that Adolf Hitler was appointed Chancellor of Germany; the *Lone Ranger* debuted on American radio; the original film version of *King Kong* debuted; Mount Rushmore was dedicated; Japan left the League of Nations; and it became illegal for Americans to own gold.

Much of King Turpin's story from this point forward has been derived from the memories of his son, Jim. In 2010, Jim conveyed his early memories of his father in these words: "He was a hard worker and a spiritual father. He was also strict in discipline; the belt was used, if required."[132] Jim also noted that he personally only remembered being

---

[131] Jim Turpin is the author's father, and he has provided much of the information pertaining to King and his family in the pages that follow.

[132] Interview with James (Jim) Randolph Turpin, Sr., May 24, 2010.

disciplined with a switch; he does not recall the belt being used on him.

Two Turpin Girls Given Away

Once when King and Bertha were away, Grandma Griggs took charge of the children. Before the parents could return, she gave Pauline and Virginia away to a family that lived at Big Four! When Bertha came home and found out what had happened, she tracked the children down and brought them back.

A Move to Gobbler's Knob

King moved his family from the Church home to Gobbler's Knob, also located on Rock House Mountain. At Gobbler's Knob the Turpins lived a very primitive life. King cut out a sixty gallon barrel and made a stove out of it. The children spent a lot of time in the woods while they lived there, and they remember the squirrels playing all over the yard. They lived at Gobbler's Knob for about a year.

The Birth of Robert Turpin

While living at Gobbler's Knob, on June 8, 1935 King and Bertha's second son was born: Robert Carlisle Turpin. Note that this was the second time King had named a child Robert. The first Robert was born to King and Nellie on October 27, 1925 and died on May 22, 1927.

To place Robert's birth in historical context, 1935 was also the year that Elvis Presley was born; Amelia Earhart flew solo from Hawaii to California; *Porky the Pig* made his debut; Persia was renamed Iran; the Social Security Act was signed into law; and the board game *Monopoly* was released.

A Move to Camp Houston

King was hired to serve as caretaker of the nearby scout camp known as Camp Houston. The camp was less than a mile from Gobbler's Knob. The Turpins moved from Gobbler's Knob to the caretaker's house at the top of the mountain. The house would one day become known as the Roark place.[133] In addition to working as caretaker of the camp, King continued working as a coalminer as well as a preacher. Grandma Griggs was still staying with the family while they were living there. Her health began failing her during those days.

As visitors arrived to enter the camp, Virginia, Pauline and Jim would run out to greet them and open the gate. Jim remembers that he and his siblings often received tips while tending the gate.

---

[133] The Roark place was the caretaker's house for Camp Houston. The house was not identified with the Roark family until many years later; however, in the telling of the family stories related to this period when King served as camp caretaker, most family members refer to the place as the Roark place.

A log house in the center of Camp Houston (not the caretaker's house). When it was standing, it was the oldest structure in McDowell County.

Another view of the log house at Camp Houston

In the center of Camp Houston was an old log house (not the caretaker's house) believed to have once been occupied by either Bertha's grandfather, Albert Church, or her great-grandfather, Dr. Emanuel Church. While it was standing, it was the oldest structure in McDowell County. At one time it served as a school house.

The old log house had an unusual feature. Some of the logs had holes drilled in them, and it appeared that horse hair had been stuffed inside with wooden pegs sealing the holes. William Church told everyone that this had been done to ward off evil spirits.

The One-Room School House

Jim's childhood memories begin with his family living at the gate to the scout camp. There was a one-room school house less than two hundred yards from their house where Jack and his older siblings attended.

One day the Turpin children were at school and the teacher had to leave for a short time. She said to Jack, "Now, I am putting you in charge. If anyone makes a sound, I want you to write their names on the board."

The teacher left, and Jack said to the students, "Now, I am in charge. If anyone does not make a lot of noise, I am going to write your name on the board!"

Everyone started making all the noise that they could. Just before the teacher returned, Jack wrote these words on the board: "Not a sound."

One December the school was preparing for a special gathering on the day that Christmas break began. The weather was cold, so the teacher asked a student who was serving as custodian to go to the school house early to make sure the fire in the stove was very hot.

The student-custodian proudly fulfilled what was asked of him. He got the fire very hot. However, the stove vent got *too* hot and set the interior wall behind the stove on fire! The young man ran over to the corner, grabbed a mop, and beat it against the wall to try to put the fire out. What he did not consider was the fact that this mop had been used to oil down the floor. With the slinging of the mop, oil was being spread everywhere! The oil ignited. There was no choice but to abandon the firefighting attempt. The building was quickly consumed in flames, and the school house was lost. The Turpins could see the building burning down from their house.

The Birth of Melvin Turpin

In 1937 while King was still serving as camp caretaker, Bertha gave birth to another son. His name was King Melvin Turpin. They called him Melvin.

To place Melvin's birth in historical context, 1937 was also the year that Howard Hughes set a new record by flying from Los Angeles to New York City in less than eight hours; General Motors recognized the United Automobile Workers Union; the German airship Hindenburg disaster occurred; Amelia Earhart disappeared during her attempt to become the first woman to fly around the world; Abraham Lincoln's head was dedicated at Mount Rushmore; Italy withdrew from the League of Nations; and Walt Disney produced the first feature-length animated cartoon with sound—*Snow White and the Seven Dwarfs.*

Some say that Melvin was born on November 10, 1937. Another source says that he was born much earlier that year—January 10, 1937. Actually no one knows for sure what day is his correct birth date. At the time of his birth, the doctor failed to make record of it. His siblings report, "When he was a child, Melvin claimed any day that he wanted as his birthday."

In years to come, King's children would recall comical scenes from these years. One such story was of Melvin. As a toddler there at their house near Camp Houston, Melvin once picked up a broom and started chasing his mother through the house with it.

Magnets!

One day a truck rolled over the hill near their house. Jim and some other boys made their way down the slope to the vehicle to see what they could find. What did they find? Magnets! As a little boy, Jim was fascinated with the attracting and repelling force of those magical chunks of metal.

Working at the Wilcoe Mine

King's work switched from the Carswell mine to the mine at Wilcoe near Gary. Since he did not have a car, he had to walk to work and back. He walked ten to fifteen miles one-way to Wilcoe, with part of that trip involving crossing the mountain just beyond Big Four. King then descended into the earth, worked ten to twelve hours in the mine, ascended back to the surface, and walked the same route ten to fifteen miles back home.

After walking home from work, King would then work awhile in the garden. After getting a few hours of sleep, he would set out to walk to work again the next morning. In Jim's words, "In those days coal miners spent very few hours with their families."

A New Automobile

In about 1936 or 1937, King got another vehicle—his first motorized vehicle since he had given his Studebaker to William Church in 1932. This new automobile was something like a panel truck. Jim remembers riding in it; it was the first time he had ever ridden in an automobile. Acquiring an automobile was quite a relief to King; however, he only kept it for a few weeks.

The Old Black Box

Around 1937, King bought the children a wagon. It was purchased in part from the tips that Jim, Pauline and Virginia collected from the visitors to Camp Houston. On occasion, some of the bolts holding the wagon together would come loose, and it could not be ridden. King would open what became known as the "old black box" and dig around in it until he found bolts to replace the ones that had come loose. That old black box became useful on many occasions.

Jim watched his Dad repair the wagon, and from that time on, Jim repaired the wagon himself whenever the bolts would come loose. Of course, being only four years old, Jim couldn't get the bolts as tight as they should have been.

Reflecting on his own attempts at repairing the wagon, Jim notes, "I suppose Dad let us do it to learn mechanics." He continues, "I often wonder whatever happened to the 'old black box.'"[134]

Electricity

At their house on the mountain, the Turpins had a windmill that produced their electricity. They had one room in the house that the children were not allowed to go into; King kept the batteries in there to store their electricity. He was able to produce enough electricity to power electric lights for the house. Reflecting on the family's use of this electrical system, Jim remarks, "We didn't keep that too long; I don't know what happened to it."

Trespassers

There was a reoccurring problem with people trespassing at the scout camp. Although King attempted to carefully keep the gate, it seemed inevitable that some

---

[134] Interview with James (Jim) Randolph Turpin, Sr., May 24, 2010.

would find a way in, avoiding his watchful eye. On some occasions, teenagers and adults would sneak into the camp and even engage in immoral activity with one another in the cabins or in the woods.

On Saturday, March 26, 1938, King turned back a group of unsupervised boys from the gate. However, they entered the camp another way. When King learned that they had occupied one of the cabins, he called upon William Church, Basil Gross, Claude Church, Frank Mileski and his own son, Jack, to help him expel the trespassers. King was concerned about the potential for vandalism.

That evening King's party approached the cabin firing their guns into the air. The boys ran off leaving their personal belongings behind. Some of them ran barefoot all the way to Kimball. Although King's actions might have been justified, this incident caused such a stir in the county that it resulted in him being relieved of his duties as caretaker of Camp Houston.[135]

Return to the Church Place

From the Camp Houston house, the Turpins moved back to William Church's house for awhile. It was at the Church place that Jim saw his great-grandfather, Albert Jackson Church, for the first and only time. Albert had a

---

[135] Armed Sextet Routs Boy Scouts from Camp, *Bluefield Daily Telegraph*, March 29, 1938.

long beard, and he always wore blue striped suits. His wife, Louise Stanley Church, smoked a pipe.

Grandma Griggs' Departure

Toward the end of the Turpins' time at Camp Houston, Grandma Griggs had been going blind, and her health was seriously failing. She felt that God was punishing her for contributing to the death of the twins several years earlier. Because of her condition, Nellie's brother, Melvin, took her to either Tennessee or Kentucky where she stayed with Melvin for awhile. Jack went with them.

About this time, Jack had become a bit mischievous. For instance, when he was sent to the spring for water, he might not come back for several days.[136] Jack's uncontrollable behavior might have been one of the reasons he was sent off with Grandma Griggs and Melvin. He remained with his mother's family for an extended time. It was about this same time that the Turpins left the mountain.

A Move to Tidewater

In the fall of 1938, King left Rock House Mountain and moved his family to Tidewater just outside of Kimball. They lived there for about a year. At Tidewater they had electricity. Previously on Rock House Mountain they had battery-powered lights, but this was the first time they had ever had alternating current.

---

[136] Interview with James (Jim) Randolph Turpin, Sr., May 24, 2010.

The children were impressed by the machinery associated with the coal mining in the area. Jim remembers seeing a big train pulling up in front of the house with steam belching from it. They could also see the mine motors moving mine cars around. Jim used to have nightmares about those trains chasing him all the way to the end of the world.

There at Tidewater, the kids would sit on the stairway where they could look out and see through the window of the next door house. They would see the neighbors eating, take note of what they were eating and think, "It would be nice to have some of that to eat." Bertha got onto the kids for doing that.

The Birth of Kathryn Turpin

While living at Tidewater, Bertha gave birth to another daughter. Kathryn Lee Turpin was born December 10, 1938. To place Kathryn's birth in historical context, 1938 was also the year that Adolf Hitler took direct control of the German military; the first nylon bristle toothbrush was released on the market; oil was discovered in Saudi Arabia; Howard Hughes set a new record flying around the world in ninety-one hours; Orson Welles's radio adaptation of *The War of the Worlds* was broadcasted, causing panic in many parts of the United States; and *Action Comics #1* was published—the first publication featuring *Superman*.

A Move to Big Four

From Tidewater, King moved his family to Big Four. They lived in a community known as Koppers Bottom. To reach the place where the Turpins lived, travelers had to go through a tunnel. That tunnel was frightening, and people didn't like going through it at night. At the time of this writing, the hill through which the tunnel once passed and the site of the Turpin home have been leveled, making room for a Walmart department store.

The first time that Jim remembers going to church outside of the family's own home was at the Pentecostal Holiness Church at Big Four. Due to the size of the family, King was not always able to take everyone with him when he went out to preach.

Jim remembers that their house had electricity and that the windows that went all the way to about a foot from the floor. They could sit in the window and watch the Hungarian vendors in the streets. One day while looking out the window, the children saw a Hungarian vendor's car open up, and hundreds of apples came rolling out. People were running up and grabbing them, but the Turpin kids knew better than to go after them. The Hungarian man could do nothing about it while he watched people stealing his apples.

Jim remembers another odd sight while living there at Big Four. Some of the Turpin children were outside and watched as they saw a guy floating down the Elkhorn River in a sixty gallon barrel waving at people!

One time at this house while Melvin was rocking in the rocking chair, he fell off and broke his collar bone. Dr. Cochran came and said, "He broke it smack in two!" He bandaged Melvin up, and the injury mended.

King had a record player there that was a little unusual. Every time he or one of the children played a record, everybody in the whole camp could pick up what they were playing on their radios! King had some records that he played with song titles like "Long and Boney" and "Hang Out the Front Door Key."

Return to Rock House Mountain

From Big Four the family moved back to Rock House Mountain and into a house less than half a mile downhill from William Church's place. It was a house that the Gross family had just vacated on Lynn Branch. Jim remembers,

> That house had cracks in the floor. On the first morning that we woke up, the floor was full of snakes! They had crawled up through the cracks! For years afterward, I had many nightmares about snakes.

King was continually killing snakes. Walking around the house outside one could see the snakes pulling their heads back into the holes between the rocks that made up the underpinning. There were also rats all over the place.

King used to tie a flashlight to his gun, crawl up under the floor, and shoot rats at night. He once killed a copperhead behind the kitchen stove in the house. Jim recalls,

> We tried to drop rocks on snakes as they stuck out their heads from under the floor. The snakes pulled back their heads before the rock landed, and we were unsuccessful.

The Turpins lived in that house for several years.

The family lived off of the land. As a daily routine, they got up in the morning and did chores—the girls in the kitchen and the boys in the gardens. The boys chopped wood and brought it in.

Their vegetable garden was located near the house on the side of a hill. When the boys were very young, King taught them to work in the garden. He cut brush for new ground to prepare for the garden, and the boys carried the brush to a pile for burning. King would call for Bertha to come watch them work. King was very proud of his children.

They raised all types of vegetables and canned many half-gallon jars for winter. One year they counted four hundred jars. King also had apple, cherry, plum and peach trees that provided fruit for canning. They made applesauce, apple butter and peach butter.

Everyone helped with the preparation of the fruit and vegetables. King and the boys picked the fruit and vegetables. Apple butter was made outside in a copper kettle. It required constant stirring. Jim remembers dodging the boiling apple butter as it popped from the kettle whenever he stirred it too slowly.

There in the country, the Turpins had no electricity. They did have an ice box, but they did not have any ice to put in it; food items were kept cold in the spring house. Lighting was by kerosene lamps.

Jim remembers that they had a gasoline operated clothes washer. To get it going, it had to be cranked. Irons were warmed on top of the stove. Some people in this era had gasoline irons.

A Warm Morning coal stove heated the house. King had a small coal mine near the house where he mined most of the coal needed for it. He hand dug the coal after blasting it loose from the seam. Wood for starting the fire was gathered from the nearby woods. The kitchen was heated both winter and summer with a coal-fired cook stove.

Green beans were sometimes strung and dried in the kitchen to make "leather britches." Apples were also dried to preserve them. King remodeled the entire house, built a barn and built a cellar to store all of these goods, including canned vegetables, potatoes, milk and so forth.

They had two cows and a horse. Now that they had a horse, King no longer had to pull the plow himself. He used the horse to plow, and the children walked behind him preparing the ground by hoeing.

When King worked in the coal mines, he rode his bicycle to work every day. When he got home, Bertha had his coffee or supper ready. Then he would go out to work in the garden.

He loved to work in his gardens. When it got dark, he would put a carbide light on his hat and on the horse, and he just continued working. He worked until ten or eleven o'clock at night. People would see the light out in the field, and everybody talked about it. There wasn't anybody else around there that they knew of who had ever done that before.

Jim recalls, "Most of the land was used to raise corn to feed the horse so the horse could plow the land to raise the corn to feed the horse." The corn was actually used to feed both the horse and the chickens.

In the summertime, the Turpins had to carry water on their backs about two or three miles from Carswell to their house. When they went to the store, they carried groceries from Carswell to their house on their backs. In the winter and spring they had spring water closer to their home. King hollowed out small tree trunks and made gutters to direct rainwater from the roof to barrels for washing clothes. They took a bath once a week, except for in the summer. In the summer they would dam up a creek and bathe more often.

Christmas Traditions

The Turpins maintained memorable traditions for Christmas. One way or another, King and Bertha made sure that all of the children received at least one present. Sometimes it was less than a one dollar toy. At other times, some of them would receive a present that they could share. For instance, they would give a wagon to all three boys, and the girls would get a doll to share.

They always cut down their own Christmas tree. It might have been one-sided, but they would turn the bad side toward the wall. They made most of their own ornaments, constructing them out of paper and foil. They also made paper chains.[137]

Shoes

Their shoes had to last until they were well used, and then King would use a shoe lathe and apply new heels and half soles. If none were available, he would cut soles from old shoes and apply them. The children only wore shoes during cold weather. They were fortunate that they had more than some folks during these depression years. God always provided, and they never went hungry.

Learning to Shoot

King taught the boys to shoot a twenty-two rifle and shotgun at a young age. When Jim was about eight years old, King took him to a hollow tree with squirrels in it. At daybreak he gave Jim a 410 shotgun to use; however, Jim wasn't able to shoot anything. The squirrels ran out of the

---

[137] Alycia Janelle Turpin, Interview with James (Jim) Randolph Turpin, Sr., December 15, 2007.

tree so fast that he couldn't get a shot. Squirrels, rabbits, groundhogs, chickens and hogs were their main source for meat.

Recreation

For recreation the children played baseball. They used a stick for a bat, and the ball was made of friction tape rolled into a ball. Playing marbles and climbing trees were also some of their favorite things to do.

Radio

Television had not yet become a reality, but the Turpins did have a shortwave radio. King ran a wire from the side of one mountain over to the side of another. He would go into town to charge a battery, bring it back, and then the family was able to listen to the radio.

The radio sat in the floor four feet tall. It picked up a lot of stations. The family listened to Jack Benny, the Lone Ranger, and other series. The children imagined in their minds what was going on in the stories. In Jim's words, "It was fun."

On Saturday nights the radio was tuned to the Grand Ole Opry. The children enjoyed these evenings. They treasured these special times with their father, seeing that most of the time he was working.

Working for the Coal Company

When King worked for the Koppers Coal Company at Carswell, it took all the money he could make to support his large family. They would draw out scrip on a scrip card,[138] shop at the company store using scrip, and when payday rolled around there would be only a few dollars left. Jim notes, "God always provided."

Old Man Echols

A Cloverine Salve salesman came through known by the name of "Old Man Echols." Over time King and his family warmed up to the aging gentleman. They had compassion on him because he lived alone. Mr. Echols invited the Turpins to move in with him, and eventually they did.

For about a month King, Bertha and the children lived with Mr. Echols on the mountain above Herndon near Pinnacle Creek. Jim remembers a couple of interesting things about his place. He had an old Edison cylinder-type phonograph that played music. There was also a well shaft on his property through which water was extracted by lowering a very narrow but long bucket-like device. A crank was used to raise the four-foot long bucket to provide water for the household.

---

[138] Scrip was a form of currency (not legal tender) created by coal companies as a form of payment to employees.

They also did a lot of squirrel hunting there. Old Man Echols really liked to eat squirrel brains. Jim used to like to eat them too. They would crack the sculls like nuts to get to the brains inside. Mr. Echols claimed that eating squirrel brains helped him to improve his intelligence.

King and his family did not live there long. The novelty of that kind of life quickly wore off. Back to the Gross place they went.

Another Old Man

There was another interesting character in those mountains. His was known by the name "Old Man Mull." No one knew much about Old Man Mull. He was very secretive regarding his past. He had lived on the mountain for about as long as anyone could remember, and no one could remember when he arrived or from whence he had come.

Old Man Mull would live with one family and then another. In exchange he would work on their farms. He also taught people how to make moonshine. Clifford Roark was one of the moonshiners who learned the trade from Mr. Mull. Ironically, Old Man Mull refused to partake of intoxicating beverages.

On one occasion, Mr. Mull baked a cake. He first tried to eat it himself, but then he tried to get other people to eat it. No one would eat it, so he threw it out to the dogs.

Apparently it was not a very good cake, because not even the dogs would eat it.

After awhile Mr. Mull started getting very old and feeble. Everyone thought that he should be back with his own people wherever they might be. They finally convinced him that he should let Claude Church, Bertha's brother, take him back to his homeland. Mr. Mull conceded, and finally revealed that he had come from Kentucky.

When Claude showed up in Kentucky with Mr. Mull, it was then that it was discovered why the old man had been so secretive about his past. Back when he was yet young, he had become intoxicated one day and murdered his wife. His daughter was a witness to the incident. Fleeing Kentucky, he had led the life of a fugitive. He had lived out his days hiding on Rock House Mountain and using the alias of "Mull."

Upon returning to Kentucky, his daughter who had witnessed the murder years earlier, agreed to take him in, but she vowed to never forgive him. His real name is not known.

Fireworks

While living at the Gross place, King found a way to celebrate the Fourth of July. Being a coalminer, he had access to dynamite. He would find a tree high on one of the nearby hills, climb the tree, and tie several sticks of dynamite to one of the upper branches. Once it became dark, King would ignite the dynamite from a safe distance, putting on a spectacular fireworks show for his children to enjoy.

**Stack and company store at the Carswell mine.
Photo provided by Alice Turpin Hatfield taken in 1971.**

The New One-Room School House

Jim started school while they lived at the Gross place—about 1939 or 1940. The building had been built on the site where the previous school house had burned down.

It was a one-room school house with an old Burnside stove in it. In Jim's words, "The students would either freeze to death or burn up." There was no electricity in it. The Turpin children had to walk about a mile to get there.

109

Commenting on his experience in that school, Jim says,

We had the meanest teacher in the world! When we started school in the first grade, for every word that you missed while reading she would give you a lick with her big ol' paddle. You'd get nervous under her teaching and miss all of them!

One day the teacher gave Jim nineteen "licks" with the paddle. Immediately the Turpins left that school and started going to the school in Carswell instead. After a month or two in Carswell, the children returned to the Rock House Mountain school and finished the year there.

In those days, the Turpin boys had a great time playing in the woods. During school recesses they would climb the trees and eat their lunches while sitting up in the branches. They also played games like "Crack the Whip" and baseball using a stick and a homemade ball. In the wintertime they rode their sleds, starting from the top of the hill behind the school.

A number of crazy antics took place in that school. One time Tommy Molaski, who had already dropped out, came back with his goat. He tried to push the goat in while the teacher, Miss Jones, tried to push it out, wrestling with its horns. Tommy finally gave up and left with his goat. On another day, one of the Williams boys came into the classroom chasing Miss Jones around while slinging a snake in circles over his head.

Years later, King Turpin and a Methodist preacher by the name of Kipfinger would hold church services together in this same school building.

The Death of Albert Church

Bertha's grandfather, Albert Church, died on December 12, 1940 in McDowell County, West Virginia. The cause of death was a strangulated hernia.[139] Over the years, King and Bertha had very little contact with Albert. His death had little impact on them personally.

Rabbit for Lunch

In Carswell, King went down a 600 foot shaft into the deep mines. The coal seam was about eight to ten feet tall. The tunnels went out for miles.

King used to eat lunch with the miners, and this one black man started bringing cooked rabbit in to share with King and a few other workers. King asked him, "Where are you getting all of these rabbits from? I live out in the country, and all of the rabbits are hunted out. It sure tastes good, but I don't know where you are getting them."

The black man answered, "Well, when I get done eating supper, I go out on my back porch. Walking across the back fence back there, it goes 'meow,' and I go 'bang' with my twenty-two rifle."

---

[139] Certificate of Death, Albert Church.

Years later, King would end this story saying, "No more rabbit from that guy from then on."[140]

Mine Disaster

On January 22, 1941, an explosion occurred at Carswell coal mine that killed six people.[141] King was part of a team of

workers who helped to recover the bodies. Without knowing who they were, King carried out the bodies of two men who were relatives-- James Church and Kelley Church. [142]

James was Bertha's brother. He was found dead in a kneeling position. The death certificates for both James and Kelley show that they were killed instantly. They both died from multiple

James Church

---

[140] Jim Turpin, Interview with Douglas Turpin, May 2010.

[141] "Coal Mining Disasters," National Institue for Occupational Safety and Health, http://www.cdc.gov/ niosh/ mining/ statistics/ discoal.htm. (accessed September 21, 2009).

[142] Certificate of Death, James Church, and Certificate of Death, Kelley Milliam. Family members unanimously hold that Kelley's correct surname was Church and not Milliam as suggested by the death certificate.

burns and fractures. James was twenty-seven years old, and Kelley was forty-three.[143]

Prior to this disaster, James' daughter, Ruth, had been having dreams of her father dying in an explosion. She warned her father, telling him about the dreams. Upon dreaming the same dream on the third night, James did not come home alive. With the family mourning the loss, King said to his sons, "Boys, *never* work in the mines."[144]

The Birth of Doug Turpin

Eight days after the mine explosion, Bertha gave birth to another son. In the midst of the family's grief, Douglas Clark Turpin was born on January 30, 1941. To place Douglas' birth in historical context, 1941 was also the year the United States was drawn into World War II.

Mine Cave-in

At some point after the January 22nd mine explosion, there was another incident in which King survived a cave-in at the mine. The rock fell in on him breaking some ribs and a leg. He was totally covered up except for his head that was sticking out. The Lord spared his life, and King recovered from his injuries.

---

[143] Ibid.

[144] Interview with James (Jim) Randolph Turpin, Sr., May 24, 2010.

World War II

When Jack was about eighteen, he returned from Kentucky and began working in the Carswell mine with his father, King. However, on December 7, 1941, everything changed. The Japanese attacked Pearl Harbor, and the United States was drawn into World War II. Within months, Jack's thoughts would turn toward enlisting.

Standing in back, left to right: Robert, Jim, and Isaac Lambert. Seated in front, left to right: Howard Lambert, Hallie Lambert, Bertha holding Kathryn, Pauline holding Dennis Lambert, Virginia holding Doug, and Melvin. This photo taken about 1941 while King's family lived at the Gross place on Rock House Mountain.

Previously the children in school were singing a few Japanese songs; however, Jim Turpin recalls that after the

United States declared war on Japan, the teacher said, "We won't be singing those songs anymore."[145]

Jim recalls how their way of life changed once the nation entered into the war:

> It was hard to buy things. Everything was rationed. To buy toothpaste, you had to turn in your old tube. We saved everything—even grease. Sugar was rationed. Meat was rationed. When you would go to the company store, you couldn't just walk in and get things off of the shelf. You had to ask for it, and the store clerk would go and get it for you. Everything was rationed.
>
> We had synthetic tires because rubber had to be used in the war. Gasoline was rationed.
>
> People could only travel for short distances because there was not enough gasoline. Sugar was rationed because they used it in explosives.
>
> Meat was checked closely to make sure it wasn't horse meat.[146]

The Birth of Alice Turpin

On June 6, 1942, Bertha gave birth to a daughter--Alice Lillian Turpin. To place Alice's birth in historical context, in those days all eyes were turned toward the escalation of war in both the European and Pacific theatres. In fact far away in Tennessee, the very land in Bethel Valley (Anderson

---

[145] Alycia Janelle Turpin, Interview with James (Jim) Randolph Turpin, Sr., December 15, 2007.
[146] Ibid.

County) that once belonged to Martin Turpin[147] was being seized for the Manhattan Project—the government's effort to produce an atomic bomb. On the lighter side, 1942 was also the year that the Disney animated movie, *Bambi*, was released.

King with His Boys

Jim remembers the short hike that his father used to take with him, Robert and Melvin from the Gross place up to William Church's house—a distance of about half a mile. Jim and Robert would lead the way up the path while King carried little Melvin. At night King would carry a bottle of kerosene with a rag sticking out for a wick. They would light their make-shift lantern and use it to light the way.

Jack's Enlistment

Military records show that Jack enlisted in the Army on May 24, 1943. He left Kimball and went to Fort Thomas, Kentucky for several months of basic training. [148]

A Move to Jenkinjones

In the latter part of 1943, the Turpins moved from the Gross place on Lynn Branch (Rock House Mountain) over to

---

[147] Martin Turpin was King's great-great grandfather. He lived from about 1783 to after 1850.
[148] U.S. World War II Army Enlistment Records, 1938-1946.

the mountain at Jenkinjones[149] near Abbs Valley, Virginia. King worked at the Jenkinjones coal mine.

King and Bertha, about 1942 or 1943

---

[149] The town Jenkinjones was named after a coal mine owner or operator by the name of Jenkin Jones; however, the town's name is one single word: Jenkinjones.

Bertha and King with three of their boys, left to right: Jim, Robert, and Melvin with his hand on his father's knee. Photo taken about 1942 or 1943.

Jim was in the fourth grade at the time attending school at Wagner—a community between Abbs Valley and Jenkinjones. According to Jim, "That school didn't even have a flag. We used to pledge allegiance to a *picture* of a flag on the wall!"

Jim continues, "The teacher didn't even have a paddle; she tied about six or seven hickories together and whipped the boys with it! You thought I was going to say she whipped them with a *picture* of a paddle, didn't you."

There was a big chestnut tree in the yard of the school—an unusual sight for those days. It still had chestnuts on it. At one time, a fourth the trees in the forests of West Virginia were American chestnut trees, but a blight imported from the Orient in the early part of the twentieth century resulted in their demise. By 1929, the existence of live chestnut trees was rare.[150] That tree in the Jenkinjones school yard could have been the last of its kind in that part of the country.

While living in Jenkinjones, King and his family occasionally attended the Church of God in Abbs Valley, Virginia. This may have been King's first significant connection with the Church of God since his days of ministry out West.

---

[150] *E-WV*—an online encyclopedia pertaining to West Virginia—reports, "American chestnut trees provided West Virginia with 118 million board feet of lumber in 1919, not counting the vast quantity of timber cut for telephone poles, railroad cross ties, tan bark, wood pulp, and fuel. The nuts were a valuable crop, providing feed for wildlife and domestic swine. They provided a tasty treat for humans, as well as an income and the joy of chestnuting for many rural families. As many as 155,092 pounds of nuts were shipped from one railroad station in West Virginia in the fall of 1911." John Rush Elkins, "Chestnut Blight," e-WV: The West Virginia Encyclopedia, http:// www.wvencyclopedia.org/ articles/ 1159 (accessed November 12, 2010).

Jack's Visit on the Way to War

When Jack completed his basic training, he came home to his family while they were living at Jenkinjones. He showed up one day outside of the house, but because he had playing cards with him, Bertha would not let him in. She held to a high standard of holiness and would not allow anything associated with gambling into the home. Jim remembers that during Jack's visit, the two of them went hunting together.

The day came for Jack to leave for the war. After saying his good-byes to his family at Jenkinjones Mountain, he drove to meet up with a friend. He left his A-Model Ford with his friend, told him that he could keep it and then departed for Europe.

Jack served throughout the war in General George S. Patton's third army, artillery division, in Germany. King, Bertha and Jim wrote him often. Whenever Jack wrote back he could not disclose his location. He signed his letters, "Somewhere in Germany." Jack served under General George S. Patton.

Runaway Horse

One time on Jenkinjones Mountain, King was bringing a sled-load of coal home, and something frightening happened. The coal truck would dump coal about a half-mile from the house, and King would go with a horse-drawn sled to pick it up at that point. The road was too bad leading to their house for any car or truck to travel. On this one day, the sled started sliding ahead a little too fast. King was afraid that it was going to run into the horse's legs. He had a lock on the runner to keep it from running into the horse, but he was afraid that it was going to run into its legs anyway. So King hit the horse with the reigns and told it to "get up!", and away that horse went! It took off and jumped over four or five hickory bars that were across the way. The sled crashed through the bars, and the horse ran on ahead to the house. In Jim Turpin's words, "The sled slid on in behind him. The horse didn't even get hurt a bit."

Miraculous Deliverance

While mining coal for his family in a small mine on Jenkinjones Mountain, King heard the voice of an angel shouting, "Get out!"

Immediately he exited the mine just before a large kettle bottom[151] weighing around one-thousand pounds fell right where he was digging coal. Jim testifies that he saw the large

---

[151] A kettle bottom is "a smooth, rounded piece of rock, cylindrical in shape, which may drop out of the roof of a mine without warning. The origin of this feature is thought to be the remains of the stump of a tree that has been replaced by sediments so that the original form has been rather well preserved." Glossary of Mining Terms, "Glossary of Mining Terms," Kentucky Coal Education, http://www.coaleducation.org/glossary.htm (accessed November 12, 2010).

rock later and knew that it was only by the grace of God that his father's life was saved.

The Fall of 1944

The next school year had just begun, and the Turpin children went to their first day of school for the year. That was enough. Their father had decided to move again! He said, "We're going to move back to Rock House Mountain!"

A number of circumstances contributed to the Turpins' decision to leave Jenkinjones. First, the subterranean coalmining was causing the water table to drop, and King was concerned about the spring going dry. Second, Douglas who was less than four years old was experiencing a great deal of sickness. Third, one night while everyone was asleep, the chimney collapsed on the house, frightening everyone inside. Bertha thought that these hardships were hitting them because they had let up on their praying. Additionally, Bertha did not like living on Jenkinjones Mountain all alone; she wanted to move back closer to home. Only one time while they were living at Jenkinjones did they get to go visit her family on Rock House Mountain. King didn't need much more convincing that they should leave.

Return to Rock House Mountain

The day came for the move. King and his whole family walked down the mountain into Jenkinjones to catch the train. The train backed up and moved forward; it backed up and moved forward; it backed up and moved forward.

Finally it made it to Kimball where they got off and made their way up Rock House Mountain on foot. They moved back into the Gross place.

Some of Alice's earliest memories were there at the Gross place—later known as Boyd's house. She remembers in those days seeing a large family Bible with pictures at the house. She enjoyed looking at the pictures.

More Shooting Lessons

King worked with the boys to teach them how to shoot when they got back to Rock House Mountain. They used to throw milk cans up into the air and shoot at them. One time Robert was shooting at a can, and the bullet bounced back off of a rock and hit him in the chest, making a big red spot.

Thief in the Apple Orchard

The family had an apple orchard there on the mountain. One day they went to get apples, and they caught some people robbing them. They knew that somebody had been robbing them each year, but this time King caught them in the very act! However, there was a problem; the man up in the tree was King's boss! King just called up to him, "Get me some while you're at it!"

The apples in that tree were not any good anyway. King just let him get them. He figured that when the thief would start eating them, he would find out the hard way that they were no good.

As a child, Jim wondered why his father did not respond more harshly to the thief. Even though the man was his father's boss, Jim thought that his dad should have stood up to him. Years later Jim realized that what he observed on that day was actually evidence of his father's strength—not weakness. To be self-controlled in the face of provocation is a spiritual virtue. The Bible teaches that evil is to be overcome with good.[152]

Near that apple orchard on top of the hill, they used to cut the trees and burn them at night. Gathered near the fire the family would have the radio playing, listening to the Grand Ole Opry.

Life on the Wartime Home Front

The war brought both fear and determination into everyone's lives. Jim remembers those feelings and attitudes:

> We had bomb raid drills. Everyone would go down into the lower part of the building wherever they were until the drill was over. We would also have what they called "blackouts." Everyone would turn off their lights at a certain time at night as a drill. You see, they expected that the country might be attacked by night from the air.

> Everyone was involved in the war effort. It was on everybody's mind. Every effort that people had was for the war. Everyone was in fear. We were always wondering if we would be attacked.

---

[152] Romans 12:21.

One night everybody saw lights in the sky. Some said it was tracer bullets. In the daytime you could sometimes see planes pulling big gliders with troops in them. They would practice over here. A lot of people got killed in those gliders; they weren't always able to find a good place to land.

Jim continues his recollection of their way of life during the war years:

I was still in school. We collected things. We had paper drives. We collected cans. People even gave up their comic books and sent them in. Everything was conserved. Nothing was thrown away. You didn't see trash dumps.

Everybody had what they called a "victory garden." They would raise vegetables for their families because you couldn't get them in a store.

We were just getting out of the depression at that time. We would gather greens to eat along the road. We would take them home and cook them.[153]

While the family was occupied with air raid drills and blackouts in McDowell County, they were very mindful of the fact that Jack was fighting on the European front. He was hospitalized over there once with burns. On another occasion his toes got frozen while marching toward Berlin. Much of what he suffered serving under General George Patton's command will never be known. In the years that

---

[153] Alycia Janelle Turpin, Interview with James (Jim) Randolph Turpin, Sr., December 15, 2007.

followed the war, Jack did not want to talk about his experiences there.

The Birth of Wayne Turpin

On August 8, 1944, another son was born to King and Bertha.[154] His name was Wayne McArthur Turpin.[155] To place Wayne's birth in historical context, 1944 was also the year that the Battle of Normandy took place.

A Praying Family

As far back as King's children can remember, their home was always a place of prayer. At daily family prayer times, everyone knelt to pray—even the little children. Frequently in these times together, King and Bertha would speak in tongues, interpret tongues and prophesy. These spiritual manifestations were not just occurrences in scheduled prayer meeting times; demonstrations of God's power were part of their everyday life.

King's children were immersed in a family culture characterized by wholehearted devotion to Jesus Christ. Years before any of these little ones had come to a personal faith in Christ, they all grew up with a deep sense of

---

[154] Interview with Jim Turpin, November 19, 2010.
[155] One family member reported that Wayne's birth date was August 8, 1944. Jim Turpin, Interview with family members, August 2, 2010.

reverence and love for Him. As Jim states it, "As far back as I can remember, I always loved Jesus."

House Church

In those days back at the Gross place, King prepared the house for prayer meetings. Alice recalls,

> I remember that Dad had a big room built on, and we had prayer meetings in there. So many people with children would come to the prayer meeting! There were so many babies that when I went to lie down, I didn't know where to lie down. My bed was covered with babies![156]

Jim remembers helping his father build the benches for the house church. In addition to King, other preachers ministered there, such as Bob Horn, Charlie Gary, Henry Bennett and Flossie Lester. The place filled up with worshipers.

Flossie Lester was a Pentecostal evangelist credentialed with the Church of the Living God.[157] King's association with Flossie led to him becoming credentialed with the Church of the Living God as well. On a few occasions, King drove his

---

[156] Jim Turpin, Interview with Alice Turpin Hatfield, May 2010.

[157] The Church of the Living God is a Pentecostal denomination based out of North Carolina. Church of the Living God and John 3 Conference Center, http://www.clginc.org (accessed November 12, 2010).

family to Winston-Salem, North Carolina to attend the camp meetings the Church of the Living God conducted there.

Signs and Wonders Continue

On one occasion while worshippers were gathered there at the Gross place, the presence of God filled the place and a miraculous sign was manifested. Witnesses said that King levitated a few inches off of the floor and glided to the other side of the room.

Even outside of the church setting, the power of God rested upon King. One day while working at the Carswell mine, a man came rushing to him with a big cut running from his hand to half-way up his arm. King prayed and ran his hand over the cut. The man was instantly healed. There was no sign of the cut, except for the blood on the ground.[158]

The Death of Bertha's Sister

On March 4, 1945, a heavy rain was falling in McDowell County causing streams to quickly rise to flood stage. Reportedly, the water rose to a level that was ten feet deeper than normal.

The next evening, March 5, 1945, Bertha was visiting her sister, Sylvania Church Willard, in the King community below Carswell. It was about 7:30 p.m., and a little three to five year old boy—Thomas Jenkins—was there who had been playing with Sylvania's son, Roger. Thomas fell from a

---

[158] Jim Turpin, Interview with Alice Turpin Hatfield, May 2010.

high wall onto a ledge. His death certificate says that the bank gave way.[159] Sylvania jumped in to try to rescue him. She and the child were swept away by rising flood waters. They were swept downstream by Laurel Creek into the Elkhorn River.

A witness to the incident, Robert Jarrells, spread an alarm throughout the community to form a search party. King, Claude Church and a large crowd of others searched all night long for Sylvania and the child. With the aid of spotlights, they searched both the Laurel and Elkhorn streams.

Sylvania Church Willard

At eight o'clock the next morning, D. N. Shrader, an electrician for the Koppers Coal Company, found Sylvania's body. She was found in the Elkhorn River lodged against a willow tree near a bridge at Norwood about a half mile from the place where she fell in. Shrader continued to search, and three hours later he found the little boy's body washed upon the bank behind the Abe Kaufman store at Big Four about three and a half miles from the point where the child fell into the flooded stream.

---

[159] Certificate of Death, Thomas Jenkins. While the death certificate shows that the child was five years old, the newspaper reported that he was three years old. Newspaper clipping provided by Alice Turpin Hatfield on Ancestry.com.

Sylvania was twenty years old at the time of her death, and she was married to Elmer Willard. They had two children—Alice Fay and Roger.[160]

King and Bertha kept Sylvania's two children until Elmer said he wanted to take care of them at Virginia Willard's house. Later when Bertha inquired about them, Virginia said they let the children be adopted by a doctor and his wife. They could not reveal their names. Repeated inquiries were unsuccessful. [161]

The End of World War II

After six years of global conflict, the Second World War ended in 1945. Adolf Hitler was killed on April 20, 1945, and war with Nazi Germany finally ceased on May 8, 1945. On Monday, August 6, the atomic bomb—developed in part in Bethel Valley (Anderson County, Tennessee)—was dropped on Hiroshima, Japan, and the Japanese formally surrendered on September 2, 1945.

---

[160] Much of this information pertaining to Sylvania came from an article published in an unnamed newspaper. Newspaper clipping provided by Alice Turpin Hatfield on Ancestry.com.

[161] Many years later when Elmer died, Alice Fay came in for the funeral. The family then discovered that she and her brother, Roger, had been placed in an orphanage. Alice said she was adopted by a family in Colorado. That family tried to get Roger a year after they had adopted Alice, but the orphanage said he was adjusted to the orphanage, and they would not let him go. Alice married a dairy farmer in Crawford, Colorado. Her name is now Alice Fay Zeldenthium. Interview with Jim Turpin, date unknown.

Jack Returns Home

The war was over, and Jack came home. He found a place to live at Norwood near Kimball and returned to working at the Carswell mine.

Jack came back from the war with perfected shooting skills. Jim remembers Jack shooting off the head of a copperhead snake with a pistol at a distance of fifty feet.

When Jack got his first pay check, he got drunk and came up to his father's house. Jack came in and said to his younger brother, "I want some fried eggs! Jim, give me some fried eggs!"

Jim went out to the chickens, gathered some eggs, brought them in, and Bertha fried a few of them for her stepson. Jack gave Jim a dollar.

Jack worked in the mines several months before getting involved in an incident that would change the course of his life for several years to come. While drunk, He and a man named Steve Stokio held up a taxi driver for a small amount of money. According to Jim, "They didn't need the money; they were just acting the same as they did while serving in the war."

Jack went to prison for his crime, serving his time in Moundsville, West Virginia. There was a coal mine there, and Jack earned the equivalent of a two-year degree. He received his mine foreman papers, and could have returned to the mines to work upon his release.

131

The Birth of Theresa Turpin

On July 24, 1946, another daughter was born to King and Bertha. Her name was Theresa Helen Turpin. To place Theresa's birth in historical context, 1946 was the year that the League of Nations transferred their mission to the United Nations. Frank Capra's movie, *It's a Wonderful Life*, was also released in this same year.

Bertha holding Theresa, Virginia standing beside her, and Alice in front.

Move to William Church's Place

King and his family lived at the Gross place (later known as Boyd Church's place) on the mountain until Bertha's father, William Church, asked them to move in with him. They stayed with William for about a year.

The Roarks

Clifford Roark and his family lived just over the ridge from William Church's house. Jim has several interesting memories about the Roark family. Clifford was a coalminer, moonshiner and a barber. He would cut everybody's hair for free. He also had a bicycle at his house; in fact, the first time Jim ever rode a bicycle was there at the Roark house.

Jim also remembers that Mr. Roark had two teenage daughters. They used to climb up on the roof and wave at airplanes as they flew over. Some pilots would see the young ladies and circle back around. They would circle again and again.

Move to Laurel Hollow

Around 1947 King moved the family to Laurel Hollow near the air shaft for the mines. The air shaft at that location had the largest motorized ventilation fan in the world.

King's house there at Laurel Hollow was one of the few places where the family had electricity. Years earlier they had electricity for one year at Tidewater and for another year at Big Four. Earlier they also had electricity via a direct current system that included a windmill and batteries. Here at Laurel they once again had alternating current.

At Laurel they had a "Jenny" (a mule) that they had brought with them from Rock House Mountain. It would try to brush its riders off against a barbed wire fence. One time it threw Robert off, and he went flying over its head into the creek. On another occasion, they tried to pull logs across the river with it. That mule wouldn't move. According to Jim, they thought about building a fire under it.

While living there at Laurel, King took his boys over the mountain to go camping at Pinnacle Creek. Jim remembers that overnight adventure as the first time his father had ever taken them camping.

Jack Turpin's Prison Break

Around 1947, Jack was out with a prison work crew in Moundsville. He noticed that none of the guards were looking his way, so he decided to just walk away. Thus began his long trek, walking from Moundsville to McDowell County—a distance of nearly three-hundred miles.

While on his journey, Jack met up with a stray dog. That dog became his friend. They hid out together in a barn and fed on the corn that the farmer had stored away. Whenever that dog would bark after eating, kernels of corn would come shooting out of his mouth like pellets.

As they traveled further south, Jack caught a ride with someone, but he was not able to take the dog with him. In years to come, Jack would recall his parting from that dog as a sad moment.

A number of days passed. Bertha was outside of the house at Laurel Hollow when she heard a voice calling from the woods at the edge of the field.

"Bertha!"

When she saw that it was a man calling out to her, she ignored him, thinking that he was flirting with her. But the man called out again, "Bertha!"

Then she realized who it was. It was Jack.

Being a fugitive, Jack did not want to endanger his family by staying with them, so he chose to make his home in the woods a short distance from the family's home just above Laurel Hollow.

There on the slopes of the mountain he built the first of two underground houses. That house proved to be inadequate, so he built a second one that was more suitable. This second home was equipped with a wood-burning stove. Ventilation for the stove was facilitated with a stack coming out of the ground under the cover of the thick foliage of an evergreen tree.

While hiding out in the woods, Jack started making moonshine. He set up a tent in a remote area on the mountain and constructed a still. After making the moonshine, Clifford Roark would sell it. Jack would also look out over the hills to see if he could spot columns of smoke, indicating the location of other stills.

The Birth of Linda Turpin

On March 10, 1948, another daughter was born to King and Bertha. Her name was Linda Gale Turpin. To place Linda's birth in historical context, 1948 was the year that Warner Brothers produced the first color newsreel. It was also the year that Israel gained independence and recognition as a nation. In October of this same year, Virginia became the first of King's children to get married.[162]

The Death of William Church

Early in 1949, William Church, became very ill and moved in with King and Bertha at Laurel. Alice remembers the sound of her Grandpa Church struggling through his final night. Finally, on February 8, 1949, Bertha's father, William Isaac Church, died from a cerebral hemorrhage.[163] Knowing that William never made an open profession of faith in Christ brought an added element of sadness to his death.

---

[162] "Obituaries," Fostoria.org, http:// www.fostoria.org/ CalBits/ Obituaries/ archive/ 2000 /a_b.html#47 (accessed November 11, 2010).
[163] Certificate of Death, William Isaac Church.

Shortly after William's death, King was in the house alone. With no one else around, a demon spirit attacked him. King began to rebuke the spirit in the name of the Father, the Son and the Holy Ghost. The demon departed.

King felt that the entity was the same spirit that had oppressed and tormented William in his final days. When William died, the demon lingered in the house until King took authority over it. Once the spirit left, it never returned.[164]

The Birth of Sandra Dale Turpin

On June 6, 1949, another daughter was born to King and Bertha. Her names was Sandra Dale Turpin. To place Sandra's birth in historical context, 1949 was also the year that Pittsburgh's KDKA-TV--the first local television in the United States--went on the air; the Volkswagen Beetle was introduced in the United States; and George Orwell's book, *Nineteen Eighty-Four*, was published. Later in the same month as Sandra's birth, another of King's daughters, Pauline, married.

King's Two-Door 1934 Ford

Since the time when King owned a panel truck for a few weeks in 1936 or 1937, he had been without a vehicle. If anyone in the family needed to go anywhere, they either walked or rode a bicycle. King rode a bicycle to work five

---

[164] Interview with Alice Turpin Hatfield, November 19, 2010.

miles each way every day. The children either walked or rode bikes two and a half miles each way to catch the school bus.

Then in the summer of 1949 or 1950, his brother-in-law, Claude Church, took him to town to find a car. He bought a two-door 1934 Ford with $100 he had just received as summer vacation pay from the coal company. The car was dull black and had bucket seats up front.

When they were waiting for their Dad to bring the car home, Doug, Melvin, Robert and Wayne went out to sit by the road on the side of the bank. They watched and waited until finally they saw a car coming up the road. Doug describes what they saw:

> Here came a drunk man driving up the road taking up both sides of the road and almost going into the ditch! We ran for the hills! We weren't going to let ourselves get run over. We peeked out behind the trees and said, 'That's our Dad coming up the road!'

> He wasn't drunk or anything, but that was the first time he had driven a car in a long time. We ran up the road, chased the car, and he stopped up in front of the house. We were all excited, looking at it and everything.[165]

Throughout their growing up years, the children did not go to church much even though their father was a preacher. Transporting a family as large as theirs was quite a problem.

---

[165] Jim Turpin, Interview with Douglas Turpin, May 2010.

Now that King had a car, he was able to take his family to church more frequently.[166]

It was very interesting how he and Bertha managed to pack the children into that two-door Ford. They had a system. The bigger ones climbed into the back seat first. Then the middle-sized children sat on the laps of the bigger ones. On the third layer, the smallest children sat on the laps of the middle-sized children who sat on the laps of the bigger children.[167] With everyone loaded, they occasionally attended church in Eckman—Flossie Lester's church.

King's Helpers in the Garden

King loved his children and took pride in them. King's daughter, Linda, recalls times working in the garden with her father at Laurel Hollow:

> Dad used to call me "Pocahontas" because I had long straight black hair. He also called me "Indian."

> Back in Laurel Hollow, when some of us kids were little, we always wanted to help Dad in his garden. Sometimes he would want to go and pick the bugs off of his plants, so as kids we wanted to do it too. So he gave us a can of

---

[166] Jim notes that the family's church attendance picked up during his junior high school years.

[167] Jim Turpin, Interview with Alice Turpin Hatfield, May 2010.

water each, and we would pick the bugs off. But we picked off the lady bugs.[168]

Lady bugs are generally considered helpful to gardens.

The Family's First Television

About 1950 King bought the family a 17 inch black and white television at the company store. It cost over $500. Jim, Robert and Melvin built an antennae tower out of a twenty foot pipe and set it up in an oak tree at the top of the mountain. They ran 5,000 feet of army communication cable from the tower down to their home in the hollow.

The only television station in West Virginia at the time was in Huntington—channel five.[169] With the use of a map, they determined the general direction in which to point the antennae, but to be more precise they worked out an ingenious plan. One of the boys would climb their homemade tower to slowly rotate the antennae while the others monitored the signal at the television set. When the image seemed just about right, they would yell at one of the other brothers out in the yard who had the gun. At that moment he would aim and fire the gun at a stub of a dead tree that was positioned at the top of the mountain only a few hundred yards from the tower. When the brother in the tower would hear the bullet strike the stub, it was then that

---

[168] Jim Turpin, Interview with Linda Turpin, May 2010.
[169] The Huntington television station later moved to channel three.

he would stop rotating the antennae and tighten it up to hold it in place.

Jim bought so much equipment for the system from Bristol Radio Supply Company in Bristol, Tennessee that they drove a truck up to Laurel just to see if the Turpins needed any more supplies. They thought that Jim was a distributor.

The Birth of Roger Turpin

On April 13, 1951, one more child was born to King and Bertha. He would be Bertha's last baby. His name was Roger Allen Turpin. To place Roger's birth in historical context, 1951 was also the year that the city of Seoul, Korea was captured by North Korean forces and later reoccupied by United Nations forces; the comic strip, *Dennis the Menace*, was introduced to America; *I Love Lucy* made its television debut; and direct dial coast-to-coast telephone service was launched in the United States.

The Death of Uncle Frank

Later in the same year as Roger's birth, far away in Tennessee, King's uncle, Frank, cut his foot while mowing grass. Frank and Laura never went to the doctor, so Frank refused to seek medical attention. Gangrene set in, and Frank died on August 4, 1951. He is buried in the cemetery beside Solway Church of God (formerly known as Providence Church of God).

Wanted

In 1952, Jack had been in hiding for about four or five years. When Jim was preparing for his high school graduation that same year, Jack gave him a haircut in his subterranean abode. Although Jack's life had been outside the boundaries of the law, Jim had a respect for his elder half-brother. He had always looked up to Jack.

There was a bank robbery in Keystone, West Virginia. Somehow the name "James Turpin" became associated with the incident as a suspect. The FBI showed up in Laurel Hollow and began to question King.

"Do you know a James Turpin?"

King thought for a moment. "No, I can't say that I know a James Turpin. I knew a James Church, but he is dead."

Jim stood nearby hearing all of this. He knew that *his* name was James Turpin, but he kept his mouth shut. He also knew that he wasn't involved in any bank robbery. With the federal agent standing there, it did not occur to King that Jim's name was James. Neither did it occur to King that the officer might have been looking for Jack, whose full name was James Jackson Turpin. Jack was in fact that man for whom they were searching; however, a few days later the real robbers were captured. Jack was not involved.

One day when Jack was at the house in Laurel Hollow secretly visiting with the family, a neighbor walked in the front door unannounced. There was Jack sitting in the front room beside Jim, but evidently the woman did not notice him. Jack's immediate concern, of course, was that he not be spotted. He and Jim discreetly got up and went into a back room. There Jack gave Jim his jacket and asked him to put it on. Jim went back into the front room wearing Jack's jacket and sat down where Jack had been sitting. Should the neighbor do a double-take, hopefully she would think that the person she initially saw was Jim, not Jack. This disguise combined with the dim lighting in the room seemed to have worked.

Not long afterwards, the FBI somehow found out that Jack had in fact been at the Turpin home. Early one morning before daybreak while everyone was still asleep, the front door of King's house was suddenly forced open, and armed federal agents came storming in. Jim was lying in his bed pretending to be asleep and saw it all happen. They searched from room to room, but Jack was not there. However, the agents did confiscate various items that belonged to him or that indicated his relationship with the family.

Jack had been staying with a friend some distance away. The FBI tracked him there. They surrounded the house, and Jack came out with his hands up and without resistance.

They put Jack on bread and water for his first six months back in prison. He wrote and told his family that he was on "red and white." Jim reports that they knew what he meant. The original prison sentence was for ten years, but even with Jack's "prison break," he only served a total of seven years of that sentence.

The 1953-1956 Transition Begins

In 1953 a sequence of events were set in motion that eventually resulted in the family's move to Ohio in 1956. King worked at the Carswell mine until it closed in 1953. The tunnels of the deep Carswell mine had made contact with the tunnels of the Keystone mine. Since the two tunnel systems had connected, it was no longer necessary to continue both operations. Consequently, the coal company decided to shut down the Carswell mine and manage all of the work from the Keystone location.

After the Carswell shut-down, King couldn't get a steady job in the mines anymore due to a lung condition that had developed from breathing in coal dust for so many years. He could only work at small mines and timbering jobs. Over the next three years, King moved his family three times: from Laurel back to Rock House Mountain, from Rock House Mountain to Big Four, and from Big Four back to Laurel.

A Visit to Ohio

By 1952, Virginia and her husband had already moved to northern Ohio. It did not take long before King wanted to go visit her. With Jim offering the use of his 1951 Ford truck, King, Jim, Robert, Melvin and Joe Graham loaded up and started out on a northward journey of three hundred eighty miles. Jim drove up, with Joe agreeing to drive back.

Throughout the years of King's life, he had seen variations in geography that most mountaineers had never even imagined. He had grown up in the rolling hill country of East Tennessee. He had traveled east to west and west to east the full width of the Great Plains. He had lived and worked in the deserts out West, and for roughly thirty years he had been familiar with the mountains of Kentucky and West Virginia. However, his sons—Jim, Robert and Melvin—were not prepared for what they were about to see. Up to this point, the mountains of West Virginia, western Virginia and North Carolina were all that these young men had ever known or seen.

Jim was driving. The journey took them through Logan, West Virginia and up Route Ten all the way to Huntington, West Virginia. At Huntington they crossed the Ohio River and followed the river downstream along the Ohio shoreline on Route Fifty-two until they reached Portsmouth, Ohio. At Portsmouth they turned north on Route Twenty-three.

Not far north of Portsmouth, Jim was amazed at the flat terrain in front of him. He drove on and on, but the panorama remained unchanged. "I'll be glad when we finally get off of this mountain!" Jim thought to himself. "When are we going to get to the other side of this mountain?"

Then it dawned on Jim; they were not on top of a mountain! They were on a vast plain that stretched one hundred thirty miles north to Lake Erie and over a thousand miles west to the Rocky Mountains! Jim, Robert and Melvin had never seen such a sight.

After visiting King's daughter, Virginia, they departed from Bettsville, Ohio and began the long trek back south. Joe Graham was driving; Jim was lying down in the back of the truck.

After awhile, Joe called out, "Jim! Are you sure we're on the right road? I don't see any of these towns on the map!"

"Are you on Route Twenty-three?" Jim responded.

"Yes. We're on Route Twenty-three."

"Go on, you're alright," Jim said with assurance.

A little while later, Joe called out again, "Jim! Are you sure we are on the right road? I don't see this town on the map either!" They could hear a band playing.

Jim sat up and looked around. They were coming into a city, and a parade of some sort was going on. A marching band was nearby.

"Where are we?" Jim thought.

It was then that they saw a sign that read, "Toledo City Limits."

"Turn around! We're going the wrong direction!" Jim shouted. They had driven *north* on Route Twenty-three, not south—one hour's drive in the wrong direction!

Having lost so much time with the wrong turn, they decided to find short-cuts wherever they could to try to make up for the lost time. As a result of all of their "short-cuts," they finally arrived home twenty-four hours later. The return trip took twice as long as the outgoing trip to Ohio!

Jack's Release from Prison

When Jack was released from prison, he first returned to Kimball. There he tried to reclaim personal possessions that had been confiscated at the time of his arrest. The chief of police, Harry Franklin, refused to return his belongings. As Jim reports, Jack told Mr. Franklin "what he thought of him" and then left the state.[170] From Kimball Jack moved directly to Bettsville, Ohio where he married in April of 1954 and lived for the rest of his life.

Tent Revivals

Although King and Bertha's children had been exposed to the Gospel all of their lives, eventually they would need to discover their own faith in Christ. As their children approached adulthood, King and Bertha continued to provide them opportunities to experience salvation.

One night in 1952 or 1953, King was ministering at Rufus Milam's church in Landgraff, West Virginia. In that service, King delivered a message in tongues followed by an

---

170 Interview with Jim Turpin, 2010.

interpretation. In the interpretation, King said, "Soon you will see mighty works of God performed."

Within days, a Church of God evangelist named Thea Jones came to Brushfork outside of Bluefield and set up his tent for a series of revival meetings. King and Bertha took several of their children with them to one of these services; Jim was among them. It is estimated that over five thousand people were in attendance. There they saw the fulfillment of the prophecy King had given several days earlier. Many miraculous healings took place as the evangelist prayed over them.

In April of 1953, Thea Jones moved his revival tent to Mallory, not far from Logan, West Virginia. Jim attended one of the services. The altar call was given, and Jim went forward in response. Initially, he felt nothing, but as he left the main tent to walk toward the prayer tent, he felt the Spirit of God come upon him. He knew that in that moment, he had been saved. It was King and Bertha's prayer that all of their children be saved.

In this transitional season, while many in the family were being uprooted from their West Virginia homeland, Jim was becoming more established. In June of 1954, Jim married and settled in McDowell County.

The Lane House Fire

One day in October of 1955 while King still lived in Laurel Hollow, a traumatized woman named Mrs. Estill

Lane showed up. She was carrying an injured fourteen-month old boy, and she had first and second degree burns on her head and face. Her house had caught fire, and she had walked seven miles from her remote mountain home at the head of Laurel Creek seeking help.

King drove Mrs. Lane and the child to the hospital in Welch. The doctors reported that the child had suffered first and second degree burns on his arms and hands.

Another child who was only one-month old perished in that house fire. Her name was Kathy Lane, daughter of Mr. and Mrs. Powell Lane. The two women were sisters, the two husbands were brothers, and they shared a home there at the head of Laurel Creek. The two sisters had been washing clothes on the porch when the fire broke out inside from a heating stove. Mrs. Estill Lane was able to reach her son, but the flames drove her sister back when she tried to enter the bedroom.[171]

Departure

King's effort to assist the Lane family in October of 1955 was one of the final documented incidents of his life in West Virginia prior to his departure from the state. In November, Kathryn married, and then the remainder of the family made their move to Ohio.

---

[171] "Mountain Home Tragedy: One Baby Dead, Mother Carries Another Seven Miles." *Charleston Daily Mail*, Charleston, West Virginia, Thursday, October 27, 1955, page 33.

Children of King and Nellie Turpin

Jack Turpin   Pauline Turpin   Virginia Turpin

Not Pictured: Pearl, Robert, Willie, Edward and Edgar

Children of King and Bertha Turpin

Jim Turpin   Robert Turpin   Melvin Turpin

(continued)

Children of King and Bertha Turpin
(continued)

Kathryn Turpin

Doug Turpin

Alice Turpin

Wayne Turpin

Theresa Turpin

Linda Turpin

Sandra Turpin

Roger Turpin

151

Chapter 5

Life in Ohio

King moved the remainder of his family to Ohio in 1956. Only Jim remained in West Virginia. The Turpins initially lived in Kansas, Ohio—a small unincorporated community in the northwestern part of the state. On Jim's first visit from West Virginia, that is where the family was living.

King and Bertha's first house in Kansas, Ohio in 1957. Pictured on porch left to right: Betty Jean Rose Turpin (Jim's wife), Sandra, and Buddy Rose (Betty's brother).

King and Bertha in Ohio

From Kansas they moved to various other places not far away, including Rising Sun and Route 635. The home place there at Route 635 became known simply as "Six-thirty-five." It was a large white farmhouse. At some point in this season of the family story, Alice married and moved to New York.

King with His Children

Linda recalls times with her father while living at Six-thirty-five:

When we moved to Ohio at Six-thirty-five, Daddy had a very large garden. Every time we would want to go out and talk to Daddy, he would be out hoeing his garden after he got home from work. Every time he would see us approaching him, he would stop hoeing and lean on his hoe. He would always have such a big smile as he watched us approach him.

We would talk to him, and he would just listen to what we had to say. Then we would go on our way, and he would go back to work. That really stood out in my mind, how he always took time for us.[172]

As the children grew older, King gathered his children around his feet, got out his guitar and played songs. Among other tunes, he sang a song about the "Ground Hog." The song was also called "The Ground Hog Hunt." It was a

---

[172] Jim Turpin, Interview with Linda Turpin, May 2010.

popular Appalachian folk song in the early twentieth century.

Ground Hog

(Author Unknown)

Shoulder up your gun and whistle up your dog, (2x)
We're off to the woods for to catch a ground hog
Ground hog, ground hog

Too many rocks and too many logs, (2x)
Too much trouble to hunt ground hogs,
Ground hog, ground hog

He's in here boys, the hole's wore slick, (2x)
C'mon, Sam with your forked stick,
Ground hog, ground hog

Stand back, boys, and let's be wise, (2x)
I think I see his beady little eyes,
Ground hog, ground hog

Here comes Sam with a ten foot pole, (2x)
Twist that whistle pig outta his hole,
Ground hog, ground hog

Work, boys, work just as hard as you can tear, (2x)
The meat'll do to eat and the hide'll do to wear,
Ground hog, ground hog

Up come Sal with a snigger and a grin, (2x)
Ground hog grease all over her chin,
Ground hog, ground hog

The children screamed and the children cried, (2x)
"I love that ground hog cooked or fried!"
Ground hog, ground hog

You eat up the meat then you save the hide, (2x)
Makes the best shoestring that ever was tied,
Ground hog, ground hog

Look at them fellers, they're about to fall, (2x)
Eatin' till their britches won't button at all,
Ground hog, ground hog

Little piece of cornbread laying on the shelf, (2x)
If you want any more you can sing it yourself,
Ground hog, ground hog[173]

King made up his own verses to the Ground Hog song using the names of some of his children. He also kept them very entertained doing various other things to get them laughing. In Linda's words, "Daddy was so good with us kids."

Alice recalls an occasion in 1959 that demonstrated his love toward his children:

It is funny how the little things mean so much. I was married, living in New York, and was visiting Mom, Dad, and my siblings still at home. Sometime during the visit, Dad wanted us kids to all line up. I thought he was

---

[173] "Ground Hog," The ToneWay Project: Helping People Play Music, http://toneway.com/ songs/ ground-hog (accessed November 12, 2010). People would often make up their own lyrics for this song.

going to have us line up by height, as he so often did in the past. We referred to this as Dad's stair-steps. We did as he asked, and he came down the line, placing something in our hands. When I looked, there was money in my hand; just a small amount. I looked at Dad and told him, "I can't take this."

Theresa, Linda, Sandra and Roger

I knew that they didn't have money to share. He patted me on the head and said, "I want you to have it."

I nodded my head and choked back the tears because I knew this was his way of saying, "I love you."

I love you too, Dad.

King pastored a church below the house on Route 635. He preached, and Bertha played the organ. Brother Belcher, who would later become their pastor, came over to minister at times.

Early one Sunday morning, King got up and went down to the church to start the heating stove to warm up the building in preparation for the morning service. Later the boys went down there to check on the fire. The stove had caught on fire and had burned its way all the way down through the church floor! It fell down to the ground, but the fire had gone out. It was a wonder that the church did not burn down.[174]

Robert had a metal detector and had detected something metal beneath the dirt floor of the basement of the house at Six-thirty-five. He and his brothers started digging. After they had dug down about six feet, they claimed to have struck gold. Nothing more was ever heard about this supposed find. Presumably whatever they found must not have been gold after all.

Two Marriages in 1960

1960 brought two more marriages in the Turpin family. In May, Melvin got married, and in June it was Robert. After marrying, Robert and his bride settled on a piece of property in Burgoon, Ohio that would soon become a frequent gathering place for the family.

---

[174] Jim Turpin, Interview with Melvin Turpin, May 2010.

King's Move to Burgoon

From Six-thirty-five the family moved to a house in Burgoon located behind Robert Turpin's place.[175] The house was originally a garage, but it had been renovated to make a suitable home for King and his family.

The Cuban Missile Crisis

In October of 1962 a frightening sequence of events unfolded. On the fourteenth, a United States reconnaissance

Doug Turpin in the Airborne Division

photo revealed that Soviet missile bases were under construction in Cuba. President John F. Kennedy demanded that the Soviets dismantle the missile bases and remove all offensive weapons. A blockade was also initiated against Soviet shipments into Cuba. The U.S. government had little hope that the Soviets would agree to their demands; therefore, the nation's military was preparing for a military confrontation.

At this time, King's son, Douglas, was in the Airborne Division. At the peak of this crisis, the men of Doug's

---

[175] Location of the Burgoon house: Latitude: 41°15'57.85"N Longitude: 83°15'16.39"W.

division were on planes ready to attack. If the order were to be given, Doug and his division would parachute into Cuba. No one knew for sure whether the order would come or not.

King, Bertha and most of their children were in Ohio. Jim and his family were in West Virginia. In the midst of this crisis, Jim looked up and saw a very large object flying high in the sky. As he watched, he saw it break apart—it appeared to explode and disintegrate. The pieces of this falling object landed thirty-five miles away in Grundy, Virginia. Initially a report was released stating that it was a weather balloon, but eventually the truth came out. It was one of a number of balloons that the United States defense department had launched to detect incoming missiles.

The Soviets publicly resisted U.S. demands, but in secret communications with the United States, they negotiated a resolution. The confrontation ended on October 28, 1962 when an agreement was reached to dismantle the nuclear weapons and return them to the Soviet Union. In exchange, the United States agreed to never invade Cuba. The blockade formally ended on November 20, 1962.

Playful Memories in Burgoon

The author's first memories of visiting Grandpa and Grandma Turpin were there in Burgoon. Picking cherries from the cherry trees and playing with cousins in the large yard shared by both Robert's and King's households are vivid memories.

King loved to sing some of the same songs to his grandchildren that he once sang to his children. One of the most memorable tunes was "Long Boy"—that old song from the World War I era. Grandpa Turpin would sing those lines while playing his guitar, and when he finished he would just laugh.

It was in Burgoon that the author first remembers his grandfather being addressed by the name, "King." He had always called his grandfather "Grandpa," and his father, Jim, had always called him "Dad." The day that he remembers his grandmother, Bertha, calling out the name, "King," the author recalls thinking that it was an unusual name. Later Jim, the author's father, explained that not only was Grandpa's name King, but Grandpa's father's name was King as well. Jim further noted that someone had said that Grandpa's father's father's name was also King. Of course, that latter claim proved to be true with the discovery of Joshua King Christenberry in the family lineage.

A House of Prayer

King and Bertha's house was a house of prayer. Visits in their home inspired godly living. Discussions about End-Time Prophecy were enough to frighten one into God's kingdom! Perhaps it was the way they prayed that made the greatest impression. Everyone got on their knees in their living room, and everyone prayed loudly--all at the same time. They would pray on and on until they "prayed through."

While living in Burgoon, the family attended the Church of God in Freemont. Brother Belcher was the pastor at the time. King did not have a title, but he was like an associate pastor. He would testify a lot of times and minister to people at the altar. Many gifts of the Spirit operated through him. Tongues, the interpretation of tongues and gifts of healing frequently manifested through King.

Visits to West Virginia

The author remembers the excitement associated with the occasional visits that King and his family made back to West Virginia. Because Theresa, Linda, Sandra and Roger were still relatively young in the early 1960's, the author—less than six years old at the time—thought that they were his cousins. On a ride from Kimball, West Virginia to Welch in 1963, he was surprised to learn that Roger was his uncle and the girls were his aunts!

Deliverance

King's daughter, Virginia, and her husband, Curtis, started going to the church in Ohio. Curtis had been invited by Gene Moore. During one of the services, a demon inside of Curtis started acting up. He was making weird movements with his hands and doing other crazy things like kicking song books up to the altar. He laid his head on the altar, made motions with his hands as though he were calling people to the altar. Some say that Curtis actually started saying, "Come, pray to the devil! Pray to the devil!"

Members of the Turpin and Southerland families visiting in Welch, West Virginia on July 4, 1963. Left to right on back row: Jim, Linda, Betty Jean Rose Turpin (Jim's wife), Theresa, Sandra, Bertha, King, Ruth Southerland (James Church's daughter), and Ernie Southerland. Front row left to right: David Turpin (Jim's son), Randy Turpin (the author—Jim's son), Roger, Billy Southerland and Ted Southerland.

Then he started going through motions like he was picking things off of the floor, putting them in his hand, taking them to the door and throwing them out. Later when he remembered this incident, Curtis said that he was seeing little demon things, and he was picking them up and throwing them out of the church.

Recalling this incident, Roger Turpin notes, "Satan was trying to mess with Curtis' mind at that point."

Pastor Belcher saw what was going on. He went to Curtis, lifted his hands, and Brother Gene Paul went toward

Curtis to pray for him and rebuke the spirit. Brother Paul was knocked back ten to twenty feet by the demonic force.

Linda Turpin moved toward Curtis speaking in tongues, and Curtis backed up against the wall. He could not do anything while the spirit of God was on Linda.

The church started praying, the Holy Ghost starting moving, and Curtis ran out of the church. He got in the car and started to go home. Some other people took Virginia and their children home.

King went to Curtis and Virginia's house to talk with them. He told Curtis that Satan wanted to destroy him, but Jesus wanted to save him. King said that he would come back the next evening bringing others with him to pray. King wanted to devote some time to fasting before casting the demon out.

Before Curtis could get home from work the next evening, Satan tried to destroy him. The evil spirit tried to cause him to run into other cars, trees and ditches. He had to fight with that demon all the way home.

King, Bertha and Robert set out to go to Curtis and Virginia's house. When they arrived, the Holy Ghost started moving, and they cast the demon out.

When the demon came out, it hit Virginia in the back of the neck. She started moaning, and they had to lay hands on her to get the demon off of her.

Curtis totally changed after his deliverance. He was saved, sanctified, filled with the Holy Ghost and called into the ministry. Eventually he became the pastor of the Church of God in Genoa, Ohio. He was an outstanding Christian and a mentor to many.[176]

Other Signs and Wonders

Many other Signs and wonders continued through King and Bertha's ministry in Ohio. Their son, Roger, recalls a healing that he received:

> I was a teenager, and I had a hernia on the upper part of my thigh. It bulged way out. It was real painful. Mother, Dad and Robert prayed for me. I had already gone to the doctor. They said I needed surgery.

> I felt the Lord come over me, especially in the area where the injury was. The next morning I got up, and I was completely healed. I played football, went through basic training in the military, and never again had a problem with it.[177]

Roger tells of another miracle that occurred through his parents' ministry of prayer:

> Over in Kansas one time, there was this girl all crippled. Her limbs were curled up. Mom and Dad anointed her,

---

[176] Jim Turpin, Interview with Roger Turpin, May 2010.
[177] Ibid.

prayed, and right before their eyes the limbs started straightening up.[178]

One of Kings' granddaughters—Robert's oldest daughter, Rita—testifies,

When I went to kindergarten, they tested my ears and found out that I was deaf in one of my ears. That evening, Grandma, Grandpa and my Dad—Robert--prayed for me. First they put a ticking clock up to my ear to see if what had been reported was true. They prayed, and then they put a watch up to my ear, and I could hear. I was healed.[179]

Three Marriages in 1963-1964

Three of King and Bertha's children married in 1963-1964. Theresa married in September of 1963, and both Wayne and Doug married in June of 1964.

Family Reunions

In the 1960's, the Turpin family experienced explosive growth as King's children were having children of their own. With over sixty grandchildren, summer family reunions in northern Ohio became times of great excitement. In the mid 1960's, these events were conducted in public parks. Later they were held on Doug's property on Route 635.

---

[178] Ibid.
[179] Jim Turpin, Interview with Rita Turpin Overby, May 2010.

A family reunion in the early 1960's

A few of the Turpin grandchildren at a 1965 family reunion

Robert the Inventor

King's son Robert lived next-door to him there in Burgoon. With King and Bertha's home being the hub of family activity, everyone knew of Robert's inventive ways. Some of King's grandchildren especially remember the time when Robert built a full-scale android-like remote controlled robot. The author saw this machine before it was completed. It was as tall as a man and resembled the Tin Man from the Wizard of Oz. Reportedly this machine was strong enough to carry a man. A person could stand on the robot's feet, and as it would walk, it would carry the person along with it.

Left to right: King, Bertha, Theresa, Linda, Sandra, and Roger

On a later visit, the author found the robot dismantled in a junk heap behind King's house. Some said that Robert destroyed his creation because it had been frightening the younger children as it chased them around the yard. More likely, Robert probably junked the thing in order to use some of its parts on his next invention, whatever that might have been.

Times with His Grandchildren

Two of Theresa's children, Eddie and Charlene, reflect on humorous times with their grandfather. Eddie notes,

> I remember he would come out of the bathroom with his hair twisted up like he had devil's horns chasing us around. He was funny. I enjoyed the time I had with Grandpa. Miss him dearly.

Charlene recalls, "I remember him flipping his teeth out when no one else was looking to freak us kids out!"

David Turpin, one of Jim's sons, remembers times with Grandpa Turpin:

> I remember times that if he was sitting on the couch and I walked by with my back to him, he liked to catch me unexpectedly from behind and reach up and pinch me with his toes. He had very good muscle control and a pretty strong pinch with his toes. He of course would laugh afterwards.

King with horns

I remember he used to call me "long tall grandson."

He also liked to use a common expression, "I've known you since you were knee high to a grasshopper," however, I never knew what that expression meant until I was much older.

I have very, very fond memories of Grandpa. I mostly remember him as smiling, joking around, laughing, carrying on... really just a lot of fun to be around. We all really lost a lot when he died.

On a summer visit to Grandpa and Grandma Turpin's house, David remembers Grandpa coming home from work one day while preparations were being made for dinner:

Grandma had been busy for quite a while fixing dinner. When it was finally ready and everyone started taking a seat at the table, we all noticed that Grandpa was missing. Then some of the adults started looking around the house trying to figure out where Grandpa was. Someone eventually found him; he was sound asleep in the bathtub!

Juanita, one of King's granddaughters, recalls her times of laughter with her grandfather:

I remember the times I would be at Grandpa and Grandma's house eating in the kitchen. Grandpa would tell me, "Look over there!"

I would look at where he pointed and then look back at him. He always had this sweet and laughing twinkle in his eyes. I would ask him, "What?"

Then I look down at my plate and see that he had swapped our plates! He and I would laugh and laugh. He did this many times. It never grew old. I miss him.

King did more than just play with his grandchildren. Whenever he perceived that there was a willingness to receive, he took time to impart spiritual treasures into their lives. At times while talking about His experiences serving Christ, his eyes would glisten with tears, his face would become radiant, and he would start speaking in tongues. His radiance and his smiles at such moments were unforgettable.

Three Marriages in 1967-1968

Three of King's daughters would marry in 1967-1968. Both Sandra and Linda married in November of 1967, and Theresa in December of 1968. The nest was nearly empty. Only Roger remained with King and Bertha.

Linda recalls a memorable moment with her father that occurred after she had married:

I had a lot of good memories, but one memory especially touched me. I was married, and both of my kids were little.

I got my ears pierced. Mom and Dad at that time didn't believe in wearing jewelry. I thought, "Oh no, this is going to be the hardest thing I've ever had to do. I've got to go to my Dad, even though I was married, and show him what I did.

So, I went over to see them. I showed Mom first, and that went well. I said, "Okay Mom, I'm going to go in the other room now and tell Dad." Mom wasn't sure how he was going to take it either. I was so nervous.

I sat down beside Dad, and I said, "Dad, I want to tell you something. Look, I got my ears pierced."

And he looked at them and said, "They're fine Linda. Now, if you had those big loop ear rings, that would be drawing attention to yourself. Now, that wouldn't have been good. But yours are small. They're not drawing any attention to you. Those are fine."

That always meant so much to me--how understanding he was.[180]

On the Outskirts of Kansas, Ohio

From Burgoon, King and Bertha moved to a house that they bought just outside of Kansas. It was at this home that the author first remembers sitting with Grandpa Turpin for extended periods of time listening to him tell his stories and sing silly songs. He loved to tease his grandchildren with various Spanish expressions that he had learned while living and working in Arizona.

Moon Landing

On July 20, 1969, the Apollo 11 lunar landing module safely landed two men on the moon. In the span of King's life, great historical advancements had been accomplished. The Wright Brothers made their first flight at Kitty Hawk in the year of King's birth, and Neil Armstrong and Buzz Aldrin walked on the moon in King's sixty-sixth year.

A Move into Kansas

From their home on the outskirts of Kansas, King and Bertha moved to a house they had bought inside of Kansas. For a short time, King and Bertha left that house to relocate to a new mobile home, but then they moved back to the house in Kansas.

---

[180] Jim Turpin, Interview with Linda Turpin, May 2010.

King and Bertha Turpin

During this time that King and Bertha were living in Kansas, the author was a teenager, zealous to find his own mission and purpose in life. Without the author saying a word about his own struggles, Grandpa Turpin would look at him and seemingly know everything about him. With wisdom that must have come from God, King would then speak the precise encouraging words that were needed — words that penetrated the heart.

175

A Brief Return to Rock House Mountain

In the 1970's King's sons starting returning to Rock House Mountain to camp and ride their trail bikes. At times their parents would return with them. For one summer King and Bertha actually moved back into the old William Church home place.

King back at the Church place with a horse named Fred

While living on the mountain, a man with severe blistering burns on his hands was immediately healed as King blew upon his scorched skin. King and Bertha did not remain on Rock House Mountain beyond this one summer. The upkeep was too much for them to undertake alone.

A Return Visit to Tennessee

In 1972, Douglas took his father back to East Tennessee for a visit. Forty years had passed; it was King's first time to return to that region since 1932. King's sister, Minnie Belle, had assumed that her brother was dead, but in 1972 they were reunited. Minnie describes that reunion in these words:

> Well, I tell you, I thought that my brother was dead. I hadn't heard from him for years. I wrote a Christmas card to Kimball, West Virginia; I had heard that he had moved there. I sent the card and figured that if I didn't hear from him, then he must be dead. Well, I didn't hear from him at all for about forty years, but in 1972 he came to our house! The last time I had seen him was in 1932! We had our picture made together while he was here.

On this same trip, Doug reports that they had arrived at one place to visit, and when King got out of the car, a man was walking by and recognized him! The gentleman stopped, looked at King and asked, "Little King, is that you? Are you Little King?" The man was someone who had known King when he was a boy.

This Tennessee excursion took in several other stops: a visit with Aunt Laura Turpin, a visit with Ida Belle Turpin (King's step-mother), a tour of the old home place at Turpin Lane in Hardin Valley, a visit at one other home place (location unknown), and a stop at the Solway Church of God cemetery (formerly known as the Providence Church of God cemetery).

Getting out of the car at Solway Church of God, within moments King saw his father's grave for the first time. There beside his father's grave were also the graves of King's grandmother, Serelda (spelled "Rildia" on the headstone), and his great aunt, Amanda. The epitaphs on all three headstone's read, "Gone but not forgotten."

King visiting with his sister in 1972. Back row, left to right: Faye (Minnie's adopted daughter), Bertha, King, and Minnie Belle Turpin Hall (King's sister). Front row, left to right: Randy (Faye's son) and Mark Turpin (Doug's son and King's grandson).

Two Marriages in 1972-1973

Two of King and Bertha's children married in 1972-1973. Roger married in August of 1972, and Alice remarried in April of the next year.

One Summer in Princeton, West Virginia

For one summer, King and Bertha stayed with Jim and Betty in the Princeton, West Virginia area. Bertha was being treated surgically in Bluefield—hip replacement procedures in both hips. It was during this extended stay that the author grew close to his Grandpa King Turpin.

During this summer of Bertha's medical treatments, King would sit with his grandson for hours to discuss the Bible. He was especially interested in Scriptures that dealt with the work of the Holy Ghost. First Corinthians chapters twelve through fourteen was the topic of most of the conversations which took place between grandfather and grandson. He continually exhorted to earnestly desire spiritual gifts.

Bertha underwent two hip replacement procedures in Bluefield—not far from Princeton. The author vividly remembers visiting with his grandmother at the hospital and then leaving with his grandfather and parents to return to the car. While walking uphill back toward the car, the author turned around and saw that King could not keep up. He had stopped walking several yards back and was trying to catch his breath. In that moment the author became painfully aware of his grandfather's mortality. In that moment he realized that his grandfather would not always be with him.

Prophetic Keenness

In King's closing years, he gained a prophetic keenness which left an indelible mark upon this writer. Upon arriving at his home, there were times when he would look at his visitor and begin to immediately speak with prophetic precision that which was needed.

Just a few months prior to his death, the Lord started appearing to King in visions. In one particular vision he saw Jesus praying the prayer of John chapter 17. As he would tell of this experience, tears would come into his eyes, his face would begin to glow, and his voice would give way to praying and praising God in the Spirit.

King's daughter, Alice, recalls that shortly before her father's death, a message was given in tongues in church. King interpreted the message. The interpretation to the message was not what stood out in her mind; in fact, she does not remember the interpretation. It is what King said immediately at the close of the interpretation that struck her as peculiar. After he finished the interpretation, he said, "And that's it."

Alice comments, "To my knowledge, he never interpreted anything after that, because he died soon after that. He knew that his job was finished, and he said, 'And that's it.'"

Bertha adds, "Before King died, he told me that he heard the Lord say, 'I'm up here. Come on up.'"[181]

The Death of King Turpin

Here the author chooses to deviate from the normal usage of the third person. That which follows is of such a personal nature that I cannot adequately convey what must be said without speaking directly in the first person.

In 1977 I was attending Lee College in Cleveland, Tennessee. Phone calls and letters brought news of my grandfather's failing health, and those reports brought on a mixture of emotions. At times there was a confidence that God was going to answer everyone's prayers and heal Grandpa. At other moments the realization that he could possibly die was overwhelming.

The family was being called in. Driving non-stop for nine hours, I arrived at the hospital in Fremont, Ohio. It was late—long past visiting hours. There were no relatives in sight.

"We're sorry, visiting hours are over. You cannot go in," the nurse said.

"But I have just driven straight from Tennessee to see my grandfather! I am exhausted. Please let me see him. I will

---

[181] Jim Turpin, Interview with Bertha Lee Church Turpin/Green, May 2010.

not have another opportunity to see him. I must leave early tomorrow to return to college in Tennessee."

"Wait right here," the nurse said as she stepped away. Within moments she came back and said, "Okay, you can go in for just a few minutes."

I stepped into the room and was taken back a bit by what I saw. Tubes were running into Grandpa Turpin's body, including oxygen tubes in his nostrils. Grandpa was fighting for every breath. I spoke to him, but it seemed that he found it too difficult to respond.

After a short prayer with him, I looked into Grandpa's eyes one last time and said, "I have to go now Grandpa. Brother Belcher has invited me to come up to preach next summer. I'll see you next summer."

Even before I could finish my statement, I knew in my heart that what I was saying was not true. I could see it in his eyes. This was goodbye. I would not see my grandfather again this side of heaven.

But I could not make myself say "goodbye."

"I'll see you next summer." Those were my last words to him. Then I turned and left.

After a few days back at Lee College, at first there was good news. Grandpa was getting better. But the situation was actually up and down for a number of days, and no one seemed to know for sure what the outcome would be.

The call came on November 29, 1977.[182] I was in my college dormitory room in Ellis Hall at Lee College when the pay phone just outside my door rang. It was my parents, Jim and Betty Turpin. Grandpa had died.

I still remember the feeling. After hanging up the phone, I stepped back into my room, got on my face on the floor and cried. However, this sorrow lasted for only a few moments, for a sudden peace swept over me. Grandpa was in the presence of Jesus.

In that moment heaven became more real to me than ever before. In that moment I became aware that I now had one more reason to aim high for the prize—one more reason to pursue the hope of glory—one more reason to make heaven my home.

---

[182] "Ohio Deaths, 1958-2007," Ancestry.com, http://www.ancestry.com (accessed November 20, 2010).

Chapter 6

The Legacy

W hat difference can one life make? In the days of King Turpin, Jr., it probably never occurred to him that people would be reading about him generations after his death. He cared for the family that God had entrusted to him, and he ministered with compassion to those whom the Lord brought to him along the way. However, the thought that his testimony would reach far beyond his immediate realm of influence would not have entered in his mind.

One might say that King lived a simple and ordinary life characterized by wholesome living and hard work. But from another perspective, he did in fact live an extraordinary life marked by an intense faith in God. It was the centering of his life upon God the Father, God the Son and God the Holy Ghost that made his life and legacy significant.

Evidences of King's journey of faith can be found in the lives of those who called him Dad, Grandpa and Great-Grandpa. Consideration of the number of his descendants alone reveals the far-reaching impact of his days. By King's first wife, Nellie, he had eight (8) children; and after Nellie's death, by his second wife, Bertha, he had eleven (11). Of these nineteen (19) children, fourteen (14) of them reached adulthood. From these fourteen children have descended at least sixty (60) grandchildren, one hundred-thirty-five (135) great-grandchildren and sixty-two (62) great-great-grandchildren. In total, at the time of this writing thirty-three years after his death, King has at least two hundred seventy-six (276) descendants.[183]

The blessings that have fallen upon King's descendants are not the result of his life alone. The godly life that he led was largely due to the influence of his Uncle Frank and Aunt Laura. Much of what they had sown into King's childhood years did not come to fruition until he had moved far away as an adult. Although Frank and Laura would have heard of the faith of their nephew, they did not have the opportunity to witness first-hand the results of their investment into his upbringing.

The blessings that fell upon King's descendants were also the result of his partnership with the two godly women who lived and ministered by his side. First, it was Nellie, and then after Nellie's death, it was his second wife, Bertha, who nurtured the faith of King's children.

When King went on to receive his eternal reward, what did he leave behind? What of enduring worth has he passed on to his children, their children and their children's children? What is King Turpin's legacy?

---

[183] See Appendix B.

A Sense of Responsibility

For one thing, King left his children a legacy of living responsibly. Even if a person were to deny the spiritual realities that characterized King's life journey, it is clear that he was an exemplary provider for his family. He was a hard worker, and he fulfilled his responsibilities.

His children and descendants after him were and are industrious (even inventive) men and women who have sustained the wholesome work ethic that they learned from their parents. From King have descended laborers, technicians, welders, mechanics, builders, a miner, truck drivers, engineers, electricians, military personnel, professionals, accountants, teachers, artists, an animator, an equestrian, photographers, ministers, musicians, writers, an editor, office personnel, salespersons, executives, entrepreneurs and more.

The Way of Salvation

While a good work ethic and responsible living are virtuous qualities, these are *not* the aspects of life that King and Bertha valued the most. What mattered most to them was faithfulness to God and bringing others to salvation.

There is little doubt as to why King was so fervently devoted to these ideals. After generations of spiritual darkness in the Turpin family, the cascading effect of ancestral sin had been interrupted by King's acceptance of Christ. Uncle Frank and Aunt Laura had shown him the way of salvation, but it was not until King personally chose to follow Jesus that the curse was broken. From that point onward, King's primary desire was to be a faithful bearer of the Gospel. Bertha shared the same devotion. Their first concern was that the people they loved would be saved.

Before Jim's conversion, he was visiting his girlfriend and wife-to-be, Betty Rose, at Flossie Lester's house in West Virginia. Jim went out to the back porch and saw an open Bible lying there. The wind had blown, turning the pages. Jim sat down and began to read. The pages had opened to Romans 3:10-12, that says,

> As it is written: "There is no one righteous, not even one; there is no one who understands; there is no one who seeks God. All have turned away, they have together become worthless; there is no one who does good, not even one."

No one is righteous, not even one? All have turned away? Yes. People had always said to Jim, "You haven't sinned that much. You have lived a good life. It shouldn't be hard for you to become a Christian."

But the words Jim had just read amplified what he already knew to be true. A lifetime of upbringing as King Turpin's son had convinced him of the truth. It made no difference how good of a life that he or anyone else felt that he had lived; he was lost and needed the Savior. Shortly thereafter, Jim came to a personal faith in Christ.

King devoted much of his life to helping people find their way to salvation through Jesus. There were many passages of Scripture that he could have used to help point the way to the Lord, but certainly the following Bible verses would have found their way into King's Gospel presentation from time to time:

"**All have sinned and fall short of the glory of God**" **(Romans 3:23).** All people have sinned in their hearts. All were born under sin's control. The first step to salvation is for a person to admit that he or she is a sinner.

"**The wages of sin is death**" **(Romans 6:23a).** Sin destroys lives and results in death—ultimately a spiritual death that eternally separates a person from God. Sinners end up in a place of eternal torment called "the Lake of Fire." Because everyone is truly guilty of sin, apart from God's mercy, everyone truly deserves eternal damnation. But there is good news; God has provided a way out.

"**But the gift of God is eternal life in Christ Jesus our Lord**" **(Romans 6:23b).** God does not want anyone to experience eternal torment. He has provided a way for salvation from sin and its consequences. He has provided the gift of eternal life through Jesus Christ the Lord. It is a gift that cannot be earned on the part of the recipient. It is a gift Jesus has purchased for all who are willing to receive it.

"**God demonstrates his own love for us in this: While we were still sinners, Christ died for us.**" **(Romans 5:8).** How did Jesus purchase the gift of eternal life for mankind? He paid for it with His own blood when He died on the cross. He paid sins' penalty—the penalty of death, and He paid for it while the world was even sinning against Him! What amazing mercy and grace!

"The time has come," he [Jesus] said. "The kingdom of God has come near. Repent and believe the good news!" (Mark 1:15). The word "repent" means to turn around—to think and live differently after a person has been met with the truth regarding their sins. Any person can receive God's gift of eternal life and enter into His kingdom once he or she repents and simply believes this wonderful report!

"Everyone who calls on the name of the Lord will be saved!" (Romans 10:13). What is the good news? What is the wonderful report? Any person can call on the Lord and be saved! That's the good news. Everyone and anyone is invited to call out to the Lord Jesus: "Jesus, I am a sinner. Save me from my sins!"

"If you declare with your mouth, 'Jesus is Lord,' and believe in your heart that God raised him from the dead, you will be saved. For it is with your heart that you believe and are justified, and it is with your mouth that you profess your faith and are saved" (Romans 10:9, 10). Once people admit they are sinners, believe that Jesus died and arose from the grave, repent of their sins in order to receive God's love, and declare with their mouths that "Jesus is Lord," they will be saved.

Will anyone be turned away? Here is what Jesus said: **"Here I am! I stand at the door and knock. If anyone**

hears my voice and opens the door, I will come in and eat with that person, and they with me" (Revelation 3:20a).

King gave his life to carrying this Gospel. While he wanted *everyone* to receive Christ, it was his and Bertha's greatest desire to see all of *their children* come to the Lord. In 2010 the author visited with Bertha in a nursing home in McDowell County, West Virginia. While trying to hold back her tears she said with joy, "*All* of my children are saved and serving the Lord."

The Pursuit of Holiness

King and Bertha held to a high standard of holiness. The Bible says, "Without holiness no one will see the Lord" (Hebrews 12:14). What is holiness? Holiness is first something that God gives a person by freeing that person from the controlling power of sin.

Often when people first come to faith in Christ, they become aware of things in their lives that may be offensive to God. God in his grace and mercy will provide cleansing, sanctification and deliverance from the controlling power of such sins. Thus, holiness is first something that God provides, but it is always accompanied by a willful act on the part of the believer to forsake sin.

The Bible speaks a powerful affirmation to those whom God has made holy:

You are a chosen people, a royal priesthood, a holy nation, a people belonging to God, that you may declare the praises of him who called you out of darkness into his wonderful light" (1 Peter 2:9).

Holiness is an approach to life that says, "I belong exclusively to the Lord. I no longer belong to sin. I belong to the Light. I no longer belong to the darkness." Such a person who has resolved to no longer live as a habitual sinner resists temptations and does not allow compromises into his or her life.

Devotion to Prayer

For King and Bertha, prayer was much more than a religious ritual. It was seemingly the air they breathed. When there was a sickness, they prayed. If someone was oppressed, they prayed. If someone was drifting far from the Lord, they prayed. If there was a need, they prayed. If there was no need, they still prayed.

These people were the kind of intercessors who prayed until something happened. They prayed long, and they prayed hard. To use a Pentecostal expression, they tarried in the presence of the Lord until God either spoke to them or until He actually performed whatever action they were requesting of Him. To use another Pentecostal expression, they "prayed through." King's children grew up knowing the power of prayer.

The Power of the Holy Ghost

King was often consumed with a passion for the Holy Ghost. If a person was already saved, then King wanted to see them sanctified and filled with the Holy Ghost. If that person had already been baptized in the Holy Ghost with the evidence of speaking in tongues, then King encouraged them to earnestly desire the manifestation of the other gifts of the Spirit.

The Apostle Paul taught that there were a number of manifestations of power that God wants to release into His church: revelations of wisdom and knowledge, discernment of spirits, utterances in tongues, interpretations of tongues, prophecies, special demonstrations of God-given faith, gifts of healing and the working of miracles. [184] These were common phenomena in King's life and ministry.

Perpetuating the Legacy

Jesus once asked this question: "When the Son of Man comes, will he find faith on the earth?"[185] Jesus wants the faith that He imparted to His original disciples to still be active in the lives of people when He comes back. How is this faith perpetuated until that day? It is perpetuated as each generation passes its faith on to the next. Perhaps a modified rendering of Jesus' words are in order: "When

---

[184] 1 Corinthians 12:7-11.
[185] Luke 18:8.

Jesus comes, will our children and our children's children have faith?"

Parents can have a lot of concerns for their children: "Will my children get a good education? Will my children be financially secure? Will my child get a good loving and caring spouse? Will my children enter good promising careers? Will my children be happy?" These are all good concerns, but "will our children have faith?"

Israel was committed to passing on the faith. How did they do it? In the Bible, God commanded them,

> Only be careful, and watch yourselves closely so that you do not forget the things your eyes have seen or let them fade from your heart as long as you live. Teach them to your children and to their children after them.[186]

Each generation would do well to ask, "What have our eyes seen that must not be forgotten, neglected or forsaken?" Those things must not fade from the heart. Rather, they must be intentionally taught to the next generation.

The Scriptures provide further insight as to how the faith is to be passed on:

> Hear, O Israel: The LORD our God, the LORD is one. Love the LORD your God with all your heart and with all your soul and with all your strength. These commandments that I give you today are to be on your hearts. Impress them on your children. Talk about them when you sit at home and when you walk along the

---

[186] Deuteronomy 4:9.

road, when you lie down and when you get up. Tie them as symbols on your hands and bind them on your foreheads. Write them on the doorframes of your houses and on your gates.[187]

Israel was called to live a life of wholehearted love for God, and they were to make that love for God visible. Love for God is made visible through obedience, through sincere devotion to His Word, through devotion to prayer, and through an unwavering faith.

Israel impressed the commands of God upon their children by talking about those commands all the time. They talked about God's ways when they were in their homes, and they told the stories of His faithfulness when they were walking along the road. As they were lying down at night, they were talking to their children about the things of God, and when they got up the next morning they picked up where they left off.

The way they dressed communicated the faith to their children and grandchildren. The way they decorated their homes conveyed their faith: they wrote God's commands on their doorframes and their gates. They stirred up a holy curiosity in their progeny, prompting them to ask their own questions. These parents and grandparents set up teachable moments—occasions to deliberately pass on life's most valuable lessons.

---

[187] Deuteronomy 6:4-9.

King and Bertha made their love for God visible in remarkable ways. Family discussions centering on the Scriptures were not uncommon. Prolonged times of fervent prayer together was a daily practice. Ministering in the miraculous power of the Spirit was a way of life.

Two of Jesus' disciples once said, "As for us, we cannot help speaking about what we have seen and heard."[188] What have the children and descendants of King Turpin seen and heard? Some of Alice's children have reflected on this spiritual legacy, saying,

> We have seen miracles. There are so many today who have not seen that. We saw it; how can we not believe? We believe today because we have seen what God does. How can we not believe?[189]

Each generation should ask, "What have we seen and heard of the things of God?" Those are the things that must be impressed on the next generation.

Will the coming generations have faith—the kind of faith that has illuminated these pages? Here is a truth that each generation must embrace: "Our children will have faith, if *we* have faith and if *we* are faithful."[190]

---

[188] Acts 4:20.

[189] Interview with Alice Turpin Hatfield, November 19, 2010.

[190] The author acknowledges the influence of the writings of John H. Westerhoff and the teachings of Michael Ray Chapman on the shaping of much of the biblical and theological thought contained in this chapter.

Appendices

Appendix A

The Genealogy of King Turpin, Jr.

The following is a condensed record of King Turpin, Jr.'s ancestry. Only verifiable facts and estimations related to the direct ancestral line for King Turpin, Jr. are included. Research has been conducted reaching much further back in history than shown below, but the parentage for Martin Turpin has been difficult to verify. At the time of this writing, speculations related to Martin Turpin's ancestral connection may be viewed on the Internet at http://turpintree.blogspot.com.

Martin Turpin

Martin Turpin was born in Virginia about 1783.[191] He moved to Knox County, Tennessee. In Knox County he married Elizabeth Russell of Virginia on October 28, 1805. He lived in Knox and Anderson Counties, Tennessee. Martin Turpin died in either 1858 or 1859.[192]

---

[191] "1850 United States Federal Census, Anderson County, Tennessee," Ancestry.com, http://www.ancestry.com (accessed November 20, 2010).

[192] Sarah Turpin notes that Martin Turpin appears in the 1858 Tax List for Anderson County owning 200 acres valued at $500. However Martin is absent from the 1859 Tax List for Anderson

James Turpin

About 1807, James Turpin, son of Martin and Elizabeth Turpin, was born.[193] About 1830-1832, James married a Cherokee woman named Jerusa/Jerusha of North Carolina.[194] He lived in Anderson and Roane Counties, Tennessee. James died about 1862-1864.[195]

County and Elizabeth is listed as a widow. The 1860 United States Federal Census, Anderson County, Tennessee (dated July 6, 1860), Ancestry.com, http://www.ancestry.com (accessed November 20, 2010) also shows Elizabeth Turpin alone. In light of these records, it is assumed that Martin died at some point in 1858-1859.

[193] "1850 United States Federal Census, Anderson County, Tennessee," Ancestry.com, http://www.ancestry.com (accessed November 20, 2010).

[194] Someone has noted that in light of the Indian Removal Act of 1830, James married Jerusa to prevent her removal. James and Jerusa's first son, Martin, was born about 1832. The birth date for Martin, son of James, is placed at 1832 in "1850 United States Federal Census, Anderson County, Tennessee," Ancestry.com, http://www.ancestry.com (accessed November 20, 2010). In light of the timing of the execution of the Removal and the approximation of Martin's birth date, the 1830-1832 date for James and Jerusa's marriage is assumed.

[195] Sarah Turpin, citing a tax record dated June 7, 1862 for James Turpin's land in Roane County, Tennessee (75 acres), valued at $250. Tax Assessment Lists, 1862-1918, Ancestry.com. The 1864 Tax List shows James Turpin heirs in Roane County, Tennessee, implying that by this date he was deceased.

Serelda Turpin

On March 4, 1851-1853, Serelda Turpin, daughter of James and Jerusa Turpin, was born in Tennessee.[196] She never married.[197] She lived in Anderson, Roane and Knox Counties. She may have also lived for a short time out West. Serelda died September 27, 1926 in Knox County, Tennessee.[198]

Joshua King Turpin

On March 16, 1873/1875, Joshua King Turpin was born in Tennessee, the son of Serelda Turpin. His biological father was Joshua King Christenberry.[199] Joshua King Turpin

---

[196] Serelda's Headstone, Solway Church of God cemetery, Solway, Tennessee, shows a birth date of March 4, 1851, but the "1860 United States Federal Census, Roane County, Tennessee," Ancestry.com, http://www.ancestry.com (accessed November 20, 2010) census shows Serelda as 7 years old, placing her birth year at 1853.

[197] Interview with Laura Turpin Dunaway, about 1980, as well as other orally transmitted sources.

[198] Headstone, Solway Church of God cemetery, Solway, Tennessee.

[199] Joshua King Turpin's birth date is shown as March 16, 1875 on his Headstone, Solway Church of God cemetery, Solway, Tennessee. Court records related to Joshua King Christenberry's support of Serelda's child imply an 1873 birth year. The 1873 is also suggested by the "1880 United States Federal Census, Roane County, Tennessee," Ancestry.com, http://www.ancestry.com (accessed November 20, 2010).

married Elizabeth Belle Magsby about 1900-1903.[200] He married several other women as well. Joshua King Turpin lived in Roane, Anderson, Knox, Hamilton and Marion Counties in Tennessee. He also lived in Alabama. He died March 29, 1933 in Knoxville, Tennessee.[201]

King Turpin, Jr.

On February 3, 1903, King Turpin, Jr. was born in Chattanooga, Tennessee, the son of Joshua King Turpin and Elizabeth Belle Magsby.[202] King married Nellie Griggs, daughter of Merritt Henry Griggs[203] and Margaret Hettie Brown, on August 12, 1921.[204] Nellie died on November 4, 1932.[205] King married Bertha Lee Church on December 26,

---

[200] King and Belle are shown as unmarried in Amanda Turpin's household in the "1900 United States Federal Census, Anderson County, Tennessee," Ancestry.com, http://www.ancestry.com (accessed November 20, 2010). At the time King Turpin, Jr. was born in February of 1903, it appears that King, Sr. and Belle were married.

[201] Headstone, Solway Church of God cemetery, Solway, Tennessee.

[202] Social Security records indicate a birth date of February 3, 1903. However, some have suggested that he may have been born on February 2 in either 1902 or 1903.

[203] First and middle names of Mr. Griggs, source: Carolyn Griggs Moore (Email received March 21, 2010). Nellie's death record shows that her father's last name was McGrigger.

[204] The marriage record shows Nellie's maiden name as Greigg.

[205] Certificate of Death, Nellie Turpin.

1932. [206] He lived in Hamilton, Marion, Roane and Knox Counties of Tennessee. He also lived in Alabama, Kentucky, Arizona, West Virginia and Ohio. King died on November 29, 1977 in Fremont, Ohio.[207]

---

[206] "McDowell County, West Virginia Marriages," West Virginia Division of Culture and History, http:// www.wvculture.org/ vrr/ va_view.aspx?Id=11416843&Type=Marriage (accessed November 12, 2010).

[207] "Ohio Deaths, 1958-2007," Ancestry.com, http:// www.ancestry.com (accessed November 20, 2010).

Descendants of King Turpin, Jr.

The following is a condensed record of the descendants of King Turpin, Jr. compiled in November of 2010. To protect the privacy of living descendants, personal information posted here is limited. Basic vital information is provided for King's children, but the names of their spouses are omitted. Correspondingly, only the first names of King's grandchildren are provided.

The names of King's children are provided in the first column, and beside each of those names in the second column are the names of that person's children (i.e., the names of King's grandchildren by that son or daughter. To the right of each grandchild's names is a third column where the number of King's great-grandchildren by that grandchild is listed. In the fourth column the number of great-great-grandchildren by the noted grandchild is listed.

Should readers discover any discrepancies in this record, they should notify the author via the email address provided at http://turpintree.blogspot.com.

Children	Grandchildren	Great-Grandchildren	Great-great-grandchildren
Agnes Pearl Turpin *(1922-1923)*			
James Jackson Turpin *(1924-1988)*	Jack		
	James	2	
	Stephen	2	1
	Ronald	1	
	Tracey	2	
	Darlene	2	3
	Jackie	2	4
	Sharron	3	1
	Lynn	3	4
	Lorri	2	
Robert Turpin *(1925-1927)*			
Willie Turpin *(1927-1928)*			
Pauline Elizabeth Turpin *(1929-still living)*	Barbara	1	2
	Brenda	1	2
	Elizabeth	2	2
	Eugene		
	Kathy	2	2
	Louis	1	2
Virginia Turpin *(1931- 2000)*	Curtis	10	4

	Jackie	2	1
	Jerry	3	5
	Joey	1	
	Rickie		
	Randy	3	
Edward Turpin *(1932-1932)*			
Edgar Turpin *(1932-1932)*			
James Randolph Turpin *(1933-still living)*	James (Randy)	5	
	David	12	
Robert Carlisle Turpin *(1935-still living)*	Rita	4	5
	Robert		
	Lisa	2	5
	Kenneth	2	1
	Brian	3	1
	Julie	2	
Melvin Turpin *(1937-still living)*	Carolyn	5	4
	Janice	2	3
	Melinda	2	
	Melissa	2	1
Kathryn Turpin *(1938-still living)*	Wiley	3	2
	Richard	1	
	Kathy	3	

	Ray	1	1
	Janette		
	Chrystal	1	
Douglas C. Turpin *(1941-still living)*	Mark	2	
	Sherry	2	
Alice Turpin *(1942-still living)*	Harold	1	1
	Robert	2	4
	Tammy	1	1
	Matthew		
Wayne M. Turpin *(1944-2007)*	Wayne		
Theresa Turpin *(1946-still living)*	Jerry	2	
	Edwin	2	
	Charlene	2	
	Houston	7	
	Michael	3	
	Holly	1	
Linda Turpin *(1948-still living)*	Juanita	2	
	Vance		
Sandra Turpin *(1949-still living)*	Stephen	1	
	Michelle	1	
	Adam	5	

Roger Turpin *(1951-still living)*	Alesha	1	
	Keisha		

Index

This index has been provided with a view toward facilitating further research. Due to the fact that the entire book is about King Turpin, Jr., his name has not been included in this index.

For further information, contact:

J. Randolph Turpin, Jr.

jrturpin2010@gmail.com

http://turpintree.blogspot.com

Made in the USA
Middletown, DE
01 July 2023

34386690R00136